Thoughts of a Polish Jew

To Kasieńka from Grandpa

JEWS OF POLAND

SERIES EDITOR—**Antony Polonsky**
(Brandeis University)

Thoughts of a Polish Jew

To Kasieńka from Grandpa

Artur Lilien-Brzozdowiecki

Translated by
MARYA LILIEN-CZARNECKA AND JOANNA GRUN

Edited by
SERGEY R. KRAVTSOV

Boston
2016

Library of Congress Cataloging-in-Publication Data:

The bibliographic data for this title is available from the Library of Congress.

© 2016 Academic Studies Press

ISBN 978-1-61811-497-6 (cloth)

ISBN 978-1-61811-498-3 (electronic)

Book design by Kryon Publishing

www.kryonpublishing.com

Published by Academic Studies Press in 2016

28 Montfern Avenue

Brighton, MA 02135, USA

press@academicstudiespress.com

www.academicstudiespress.com

This book was written when Kasieńka, my first child and Artur's first grandchild, was born. He dedicated the book to her; however, I am sure that if her two younger brothers, Ronald and Marc, were alive at the time, the book would have been dedicated to all three of them. Artur intended to educate our family and future generations about where they came from. I hope this translation will be cherished by his descendants—my children and grandchildren— as well as anyone interested in the amazing roots of the Jews of Poland. At the time the book was written, World War II was raging and Artur could not have known of the cruel fate that was to befall the largest Jewish population in the world.

Joanna Grun

Artur Lilien-Brzozdowiecki with his granddaughter Cathy (Kasieńka). London, 1944. Courtesy of Catherine Grun

Contents

Preface

Artur Lilien-Brzozdowiecki and His Reminiscences

A rtur Lilien-Brzozdowiecki (1890, Lwów–1958, London) belongs to those people who left their home city of Lwów, but kept on returning there in their thoughts.

Lilien's life, like the existence of his native city, was shaken by two world wars. Before 1914, in Lilien's formative years, Lwów was a prosperous metropolis of Galicia, which bordered on the Russian Empire. It was a home to multiple religious and ethnic groups whose wellbeing rested on a sophisticated equilibrium, in which diverse economic, confessional, and political interests were balanced. By birth, Lilien belonged to the Jewish community, to its locally rooted, profoundly assimilated, educated, and wealthy elite. His ancestors played an outstanding role in shaping that precious culture of coexistence, in bringing to terms financial, communal, and political forces operating in the local, provincial, and national arenas. He belonged to a family that promoted Polish autonomy in Habsburg Galicia. Teenage Lilien participated in a radical circle striving to achieve the independence of Poland. As an officer, at the personal request of the future president Józef Piłsudski, Lilien pioneered in training Polish legionnaires in 1912 and thus laid the foundations for the artillery corps of the future Polish state. A lawyer and financier in peaceful times, during the First World War he served in the Austro-Hungarian army, returning to Lwów on its disbandment in 1918. Soon he witnessed an atrocity unthinkable under the "ancient regime": a bloody pogrom mounted by victorious Polish soldiers in Jewish quarters of his city. Those scenes bitterly challenged

Lilien's Polish patriotism, overshadowing his interwar life. Moreover, his inherited skills and acquired experience were no longer required as a new center of power was consolidating in Warsaw and a new elite had developed a new style of doing things, unrelated to that mastered between Lwów and Vienna. Although Lilien often felt himself an undesired stranger in his city and country, he joined the Polish Army as a lieutenant in the reserves. He also served the Second Republic as a diplomat, was able to share his political views in the press, and managed his family business.

At the outbreak of World War II, when Lwów was surrounded by Nazi and Soviet troops in autumn of 1939, Lilien left the city with a unit of the Polish Army—as it turned out, forever. He escaped the destiny of those Polish officers whom Soviet persecutors shot dead in Katyń, and he escaped the Holocaust that annihilated the Jewish community of Lwów. Lilien crossed the Romanian border, made his way to Cyprus, and was engaged by the British Military Mission in the Middle East. In 1944 he became an officer of the British Staff in Cairo. There he typed his reminiscences, a document of personal and family memories and his meditations on those cruel times when the old orders fell apart to give way to a new, yet unknown, world order.

Lilien invites his future reader, his new-born granddaughter Kasieńka,[1] to encounter her family, generations of Polish Jewry: merchants, lease-holders, bankers, industrialists, politicians, communal leaders, army officers, scholars, physicians, artists, and art collectors. They dwell in a broader Jewish and Christian world of deeds and ideas, integrated into the national life of the Old Commonwealth, the Habsburg Empire, and the Second Polish Republic. They serve their community as elders and philanthropists, as founders of synagogues and charities. They love and protect their family and care about their downtown house and summer villa. They—gentlemen and ladies—are devoted professionals and great hobbyists, fascinated with arts and sports. Through the present publication, the reader will enjoy reminiscences of this worthy life, narrated with great talent and decency, with many

---

[1]   Kasieńka is an endearing diminutive of Kasia (Cathy).

bitter notes together with delicate humor and self-irony. This unpretentious preface will not spoil the reader's pleasure. Instead, it will briefly introduce the author, Artur Lilien-Brzozdowiecki, rather than his story.

Lilien the narrator positions himself as a man profoundly rooted in his family history. One of his family's dominating merits is aristocracy, a worldly feature not contradicting their Jewishness. Actually, on his maternal side Lilien is a great-great-grandson of Majer Rachmiel von Mises (1800–1891), who in 1881 was granted hereditary nobility by Emperor Franz Joseph I for contributing to the prosperity of the monarchy, city, and community.[2] Lilien endeavors to reinforce his aristocracy by constructing his paternal lineage. He relates a legend about Mechel von Lilien, buried in Brzozdowce, the Galician nest of the family. According to Lilien, Mechel von Lilien was a German knight who fell in love with a German Jewess from Swabia and wanted to marry her: "She consented under the condition that he convert to Judaism. There was, however, a death penalty for defection from the Christian faith. He therefore left his country, abandoned his title, position, and wealth and emigrated with her to Poland, known for religious tolerance" (p. 41).

The Nierensteins, other relatives on the maternal side, also belonged to the higher strata of society: grandfather Maurycy's mother was born Wahl. Lilien tells the following:

> There is a legend among the Jews that during the First Free Elections [to the Polish throne], it was suspected that one of the political parties might forcefully take possession of the crown jewels for the [House of] Valois or the Habsburgs, and they looked for a secure place to hide them, [and a Jew] Saul was entrusted with them. Therefore, said the Jews, he was for one night the Polish king. Hence also comes his byname Wahl (meaning: election [in German]), which became the family name. (p. 23)

---

2   R. Pytel, "Mises, Majer Jerachmiel von," in *Österreichisches Biographisches Lexikon*, 13 vols. (Graz: H. Böhlau , 1957–2012), 6: 317–318; Jörg Guido Hülsmann, *Mises: The Last Knight of Liberalism* (Auburn: Ludwig von Mises Institute, 2007), 12–16.

Despite the formal and legendary basis, Lilien does not treat his aristocracy as unconditionally granted. Like his ancestors, he does his best to follow the lifestyle of a nobleman and urban patrician. Like his father, he volunteers for military service as an officer, and he brings up his son Adam (1914–1993)—a Polish officer who fought at Tobruk and Monte Cassino—in the same spirit. Artur runs an open house and is devoted to his ancestral villa and collections, as well as to his stable. He shelters the former enemy, an officer of the defeated Russian Army, Arkady Gonczarow, and other Russian emigrants. "I thought that if the revolution can bring about murder and devastation under the motto 'Proletarians of all countries, unite!' one should at least come to the rescue of the survivors under the motto 'Gentlemen of all countries, unite!' Besides, I thought, one day I could find myself in a similar situation" (p. 89).

Though Lilien's nobility originates from the emperor's authority, and it implements the aristocrat's diligent service to the Austro-Hungarian monarchy, and later to the Polish Republic, Lilien's roots in Polish history are deeper and are of special value in restituted Poland. These roots are emphasized in the story of Izak Nachmanowicz (d. 1595) and his daughter-in-law—the Golden Rose (d. 1637), the legendary foremother of the Mises family—and hence the Lwów branch of the Lilien family. The roles and meanings of these historically remote figures are manifold in Lilien's narration. First, Izak Nachmanowicz was a financier to the Polish Crown; in addition, he was a community elder and a founder of the revered synagogue. His daughter-in-law was a legendary rescuer of that synagogue from the hands of the Jesuits. Her grave became the site of a women's cult in the Old Cemetery, the pantheon of Lwów Jewry. The plot of land purchased by the Nachmanowicz family to be handed over to the Jesuits as a ransom for the restituted synagogue served the city and the state well in the twentieth century: it housed the Financial Direction in place of the Jesuit convent that had been closed down. Thus, Izak and Rose, the historical and legendary heroes, bind the merits of a Polish Jew in a unique garland which will grant respectful status to their descendants. They cast worthy examples of personal devotion to the Jewish community from which benefited not only this small group but also the state, the city, and society at large. It is from this perspective of existential duty that Lilien describes the local scenes—of Lwów and Żółkiew—to which he is historically and emotionally tied, where every stone is speaking to him, and to where he returns in his memories: "And Lwów, this beautiful Lwów, my dearest city! The city of gardens among green hills with a hundred noble towers rising toward the sky. The city of my family treasures, where not only cemeteries, but also things alive, public buildings, institutions, and railway lines told me the history of my fathers and forefathers" (p. 84).

Lilien's nobility, as well as his Jewishness, are not confined to strict definitions. Lilien's allegiance to the internationality of a gentleman is rooted in the elitist culture of Austro-Hungary. It is close to the image of a gentleman poetized by outstanding Austrian author Joseph Roth (1894–1939) who, like Lilien, was a grateful pupil of Helena Szajnocha née von Schenk (1864–1946).[3] Both young men, Lilien and Roth, were grafted with her tolerant conservatism at their French lessons. The hero of Roth's 1934 novel, Count Morstin, was "one of the noblest and purest sort of Austrian, plain and simple. That is, a man above nationality, and therefore of true nobility." Asked "to which 'nationality' or race he felt he belonged, the Count would have felt rather bewildered, baffled even, by his questioner, and probably bored and somewhat indignant."[4] Unlike "plain and simple" Morstin, Lilien is readily discussing racial features of his family, and everyone is beloved and ennobled in his lineage: "it seems that a thousand years ago, from French they [the Liliens] became Germans, then Polish Jews some three hundred years ago, and who knows if nowadays these Polish Jews will not become

---

3 David Bronsen, *Joseph Roth: Eine Biographie* (Cologne: Kiepenheuer & Witsch, 1974), 114–115, 493; Joseph Roth, *Briefe 1911–1934*, ed. Hermann Kesten (Cologne: Kiepenheuer & Witsch, 1970), 36–39, 42–44, 66, 127–128, 135–137; Joseph Roth, *A Life in Letters*, trans. and ed. Michael Hofmann (New York: W. W. Norton & Co., 2012), 14. Lilien and Roth were both related to Siegmund (Shulim) Grübel, the landlord of Helena Szajnocha's apartment. I am profoundly thankful to Victoria Lunzer-Talos and Heinz Lunzer for their insights on Joseph Roth and his milieu.

4 Joseph Roth, *Hotel Savoy; Fallmerayer the Stationmaster; The Bust of the Emperor*, trans. John Hoare (Woodstock: Overlook Press, 1986), 157–158.

British or Americans" (p. 42). Lilien describes his Ashkenazi and Sephardi ancestors with equal sympathy, and their roots are traced to the Rhineland, Padua, Leghorn, and the caliphs' court of Cordova. Lilien discovers in his family "the Sephardic-Moorish," "the purest Semitic," "Khazar," "Turan-Mongolian," "Slavic," and "Germanic" blood. Everything remains in the family.

Lilien is a man of broad horizons, anything but a *shtetl* or ghetto Jew. The break away from traditional Jewish society had been undertaken by his ancestors a few generations earlier. They were *maskilim*, secular educated Jews: the merchants and bankers Majer Rachmiel and Abraham-Artur Mises of Lwów, as well as Ozjasz and Maurycy Nierenstein of Brody. In their days, secular education based on the German language was a privilege of those Jews who sought to integrate into the modernizing society of the Habsburg Empire. In Lilien's generation and milieu, secular education was the standard, and a doctoral degree was a desired addition. In his day, the German language was no longer the main attribute of an educated person in Galicia and had lost its meaning as a single gateway to world culture. Already Lilien's grandmother, Klara Nierenstein née Mises, "was a living dictionary of German, French, English, and Italian" (p. 18). For Lilien, command of German was understandable per se, while perfect knowledge of the Polish language, literature, and history became vital in Galicia long before the fall of the Austro-Hungarian monarchy. Lilien's mastering of Polish and Russian, as well as English, French, and Italian made him an indispensable expert and lecturer, an esteemed liaison officer during World War II.

A true belonging to the wider world was guaranteed by Lilien's continuous education: first at the primary school run by Polish ladies, Józefa Czarnowska and Wanda Dalecka,[5] later at the Evangelic school, then at the "Bernardine" Gymnasium[6] and afterward with his private tutors including Helena Szajnocha-Schenk, then in the Department of Law of Lwów University, followed by the Export Academy in Vienna,

---

5   See Appendix.
6   In continental Europe, the term "gymnasium" denoted a school that was preparatory to study at the universities.

and ultimately—his self-education. The subjects in which Lilien took an interest, besides his civil and military professions, portray an intelligent person of his times: individual and collective psychology, racial theory, physics, political theory—including creation of the future European Union,[7] music, literature, art, history, and archaeology. "Sometimes I smiled with pity at myself and my 'education.' I realized that not only any engineer or physician, but also every shoemaker, carpenter, watchmaker, or bookbinder is better equipped to earn a living among strangers than myself. It turned out, however, that my knowledge of many languages came in useful as a weapon" (p. 110).

Yet, alongside his polyglot skills, assimilation, nobility, and his internationalist and universal leanings, Artur Lilien remains a Jew. His Judaism is not identical with that of his great-great-grandfather, Majer Rachmiel Mises, a founder of the Deutsch-Israelitisches Bethaus (German-Israelite Prayer House, popularly named the Tempel) in Lwów of the 1840s. Indeed, Lilien's Judaism is similar to that of the Tempel congregation, once formulated by R. Isac Noa Mannheimer (1793–1865) in Vienna. Mannheimer claimed that after the destruction of the ancient Temple, Jews carried its holiness with them; the love of God and faith in Him provided the element that unified the Jewish people and rendered it holy. Mannheimer's Judaism recognized "the historical, national side" of Jewish Messianism and "hoped for and expected salvation in this sense," while it did not expect the future restoration of the Jewish people as a political nation.[8] In addition to this mindset, fundamental to the Progressive Judaism of Galicia, Lilien believes that "the essential ideal of Judaism is the ideal of Messianism, the yearning for brotherly coexistence of humanity and of uniting all endeavors to uplift universal happiness" (p. 96).

---

7   Artur Lilien-Brzozdowiecki, "Paneuropa a zagadnienie granic polsko-niemieckich," *Nasza Przyszłość: wolna trybuna zachowawczej myśli państwowej* 8 (February 1931): 113–119; Dariusz Miszewski, "Polska wobec koncepcji Paneuropy," in *W kręgu polityki*, ed. Adam Ilciów and Robert Potocki (Zielona Góra: Śląskie Towarzystwo Naukowe im. Michała Grażyńskiego, 2009), 109–118.

8   Marsha L. Rozenblit, "Jewish Identity and the Modern Rabbi: The Cases of Isak Noa Mannheimer, Adolf Jellinek, and Moritz Güdemann in Nineteenth-Century Vienna," *Leo Baeck Institute Year Book* 35 (1990): 108–110.

Lilien's approach to the political future of the Jewish people is Messianic, and explicitly anti-Zionist: he does not see Jews as a political nation. He applauds the role played by Jewish Diaspora in the world: "The dispersion, which was looked upon as a curse, became in a way a blessing, because, while keeping deep in their hearts the Messianic ideals of brotherly coexistence of the nations, they found themselves in a position enabling them to become the pioneers of the future humanity" (p. 96).

As a Polish diplomat on his way to Palestine, Lilien observes the Zionist pioneers, the *ḥalutzim*, "with amazement and some kind of envy." Nevertheless, he does not share their ideology: "Palestine is a symptom of disease; a symptom of infection by the venom of the nationalism prevailing nowadays. It is forsaking directions from time immemorial and entering the road of false prophets of the moment. It is abandoning the road of greatness in service to humanity and choosing the narrow limited path of its own 'folk'" (p. 97).

In his contemplations on the world order that would be established afterWorld War II, Lilien hopes that in the future "they will understand that one can criticize Zionism while at the same time be deeply moved not only by the eternal Gehenna, but also by the magnitude of the Jewish mission" (p. 120).

Lilien harshly rejected constructing and tarnishing any "other" in interwar Poland; he was distressed by his own thinking about Poles as "them" (p. 99). Though not a sympathizer of Jewish—or any other—radicals, he was not "surprised at the extreme revolutionary reaction of the desperate Jewish youth, who did not grow up in the Polish tradition and were oppressed, rejected, and becoming poorer and poorer" (p. 100). He condemned inhumane treatment of political opponents of the course followed by the Polish government (pp. 83, 115), detained without formal charges or trial in the Bereza Kartuska prison as a "threat to security, peace and social order."[9]

---

9   See Wojciech Śleszyński, *Obóz odosobnienia w Berezie Kartuskiej 1934–39* (Białystok: Instytut Historii Uniwersytetu w Białymstoku, 2003), 16.

Lilien's great resentment was ignited by the antisemitism that increased in the 1930s, borrowing much of the Nazi ideology. Though unmentioned in Lilien's memoirs, his participation in public discussion focusing on "the Jewish question" was notable. A dispute, which involved Lilien, was initiated by Jerzy Giedroyc (1906–2000), a Polish author and political activist, in his periodical *Bunt Młodych* (Revolt of the Young), renamed *Polityka* in 1937.[10] The dispute was opened in 1932 by an entire issue of *Bunt Młodych* devoted to the so-called "Jewish question" and entitled *Co robić z Żydami?* (What to Do with the Jews?).[11] The opinions voiced in that issue reverberated in the broader press with responses by diverse sectors of Polish society.[12] In 1938, the polemic was continued by Ferdynand Goetel (1890–1960), a well-known author and member of the Polish Academy of Literature since 1936, an editor of a popular periodical *Kurier Poranny* (The Morning Courier), and once, in their youth, a friend of Lilien. In his article "Dyskusja nad problemem żydowskim w Polsce" (Discussion on the Jewish Problem in Poland), Goetel denigrates Jews as the cause of "the weakness of Poland," as an alien element harmful to the Polish economy, serving the interests of either the Stalinist or Trotskyist enemy. He blames Polish Jews as being failed nationalists unable to materialize their Zionist dream, as people totally detached from the Polish cultural legacy, although formally bearing Polish citizenship. Goetel's conclusion was that Jews had to leave Poland, willingly or unwillingly.[13]

Within a month Lilien published a reply article: "Myśli polskiego Żyda" (Thoughts of a Polish Jew), a title borrowed for the present book.[14]

---

10 Adolf Bocheński (1909–1944), one of the periodical's editors, is mentioned with great respect and quoted in Lilien's memoirs.
11 *Bunt Młodych* 33 (1932).
12 Rafał Habielski, *Dokąd nam iść wypada? Jerzy Giedroyc od "Buntu Młodych" do "Kultury"* (Warsaw: Towarzystwo "Więź," 2007), 177–184.
13 Ferdynand Goetel, "Dyskusja nad problemem żydowskim w Polsce," *Polityka* 15 (161) (10 July 1938): 4–6.
14 Artur Lilien-Brzozdowiecki, "Myśli polskiego Żyda," *Polityka* 18 (163) (10 Aug.1938): 6, 8. The article has recently been republished and commented upon in Rafał Habielski and Jerzy Jaruzelski, eds., *Zamiary, przestrogi, nadzieje: Wybór publicystyki: "Bunt Młodych," "Polityka," 1931–1939* (Lublin: Wydawnictwo Uniwersytetu Marii Curie-Skłodowskiej, 2008), 408–415.

This text is written from the standpoint of an assimilated Polish Jew, whose family served the country for many centuries and who feels deeply rooted in Polish history and his native Lwów. However, this Jew is rejected by the Polish establishment in the interwar period, becoming "a stranger," wandering "on the margins of life." All these occur to him despite his strongest desire that he himself and every Polish Jew feel that Poland is "us." Lilien's text, rich in names and events, speaks about its author and his views on the "Jewish question" better than any commentary; it is published in the present volume in English translation (see Appendix).

In the article, as in his memoirs, Lilien provides an impressive testimony of his ancestors' contribution to the prosperity of Lwów and Poland. Some of these should be viewed critically, as they are not supported by known records. For instance, a genealogical link between the Mises-Koziner family and Izak Nachmanowicz, the founder of the Golden Rose Synagogue, cannot be traced between the disappearance of the Nachmanowicz family from the historical record in the mid-seventeenth century and the earliest mention of a certain Eliahu Koziner, the founder of the Mises dynasty, who lived at the end of the same century.[15] Nachman Izakowicz, the son of Izak Nachmanowicz and husband of the historical Rosa—the legendary Golden Rose—died in 1616,[16] and thus could not have been a tax collector serving King John II Casimir Vasa, who reigned in 1648–1654, as maintained by Lilien.[17] The large, six-windows-wide house at 18 Rynek Square—where Jews were prohibited from owning possessions until the Austrian constitution of 1867—was not granted by King John Casimir to Nachman Izakowicz. As attested by archival sources, the house was built in 1777–1785 and sold by the Armenian merchant Andrzej Andzułowski to

---

15 Majer Bałaban, *Żydzi lwowscy na przełomie XVIgo i XVIIgo wieku* (Lwów: Fundusz konkursowy im. H. Wawelberga, 1906), 187–195; Majer Bałaban, "Genealogical Tree of the Ornstein-Braude Family" (Heb.), in *Księga jubileuszowa ku czci D-ra Markusa Braudego* (Warsaw: Tow. Krzewienia Nauk Judaistycznych w Polsce, 1931), 33–35; plates VIII–XI.

16 Bałaban, *Żydzi lwowscy*, 107, 195.

17 Lilien-Brzozdowiecki, "Myśli polskiego Żyda," 6.

Rachmiel Hirsz Mises on 20 August 1789 for 8,000 ducats.[18] The afore-mentioned legends were not invented by Lilien: they circulated as a part of his family's collective memory.[19] Actually, Lilien confessed to his granddaughter Kasieńka: "I want to tell you this, and that, though older things may be at times foggy, blurred, may be even fantastic, while things more recent will be treated more broadly. About things remote in time, I want to repeat for you what I heard about them at home, though, alongside the truth, they may be part legend. About things recent, I want to tell you the way I remember and think of them" (p. 2).

☙ ☙ ☙

No doubt, Lilien is very sharp and specific about the things he remembers. His critical remarks about many persons in his memoirs are harsh; for this reason neither he nor his family rushed with their publication until today. The typescript was preserved as a treasure of family history and memory. It was translated into English to make it accessible to the younger generations who grew up in the West and could not read Polish. The English translation was done by Marya Lilien-Czarnecka (1900–1998), Artur's younger sister, and his daughter Joanna Grun (b. 1921), who deserve separate biographical notes.

Marya Lilien-Czarnecka was born in Lwów and received her MA in architecture from the Lwów Polytechnic University in 1931. She worked as an architect in Lwów and Warsaw in 1932–1935. During her journey to the USA in 1935, Marya went to the Taliesin estate in Wisconsin and visited the outstanding American architect Frank Lloyd Wright. Several months later she joined his fellowship. In 1937, Marya returned to Poland to take care of her family obligations, and the outbreak of World War II found her in Lwów. She crossed the Romanian border, returning to the United States in 1940 on the last boat leaving Naples before Italy declared war on the Allies. She spent the summer of 1941 in Taliesin and then moved to Chicago, where she

---

18 Volodymyr Vuitsyk, "Ploshcha Rynok, 18," *Visnyk instytutu Ukrzakhidproektrestavratsiia* 14 (2004): 125.

19 For another version of the Mises family genealogy, see B. Samuel, "Helene von Mises," *Ost und West* 12 (December 1905): 792.

began teaching at the School of the Art Institute. There she organized a highly respected interior design program and was appointed Head of the Department of Interior Design, where she lectured until 1967. In 1966 she established The Marya Lilien Foundation for the Advancement of Interior Design. On her retirement from the Art Institute, Marya continued to teach architectural history at Columbia College in Chicago. She was a member of several institutions: The American Institute of Interior Designers, American Society of Interior Designers, National Home Fashions League, Interior Design Educators Council, Kościuszko Foundation, Polish Institute of Arts and Sciences of America, and The Polish Arts Club in Chicago. She authored numerous articles in her field and contributed to books and encyclopedias.[20]

Joanna Grun née Lilien was born in Lwów. She graduated from high school in her native city in 1938 and attended the Ecole Supérieure de Sécretariat in Brussels. In May 1940, when the Nazis invaded Belgium, Joanna fled to Paris, and then had to move to southern France. She found herself in Marseilles, hiding with the Sisters of St Vincent de Paul. Joanna married Charles Grun and left the sisters. The young couple walked forty miles to cross the Spanish border and reach Fugueras. Charles was arrested by the Spanish police and sent to the concentration camp in Miranda de Ebro, while Joanna, with the help of the Polish consulate, was sent to Lisbon toward the end of 1942, and in 1943 made her way to London, where Charles joined her. She worked for the Polish Government in Exile as a secretary. The Gruns moved to Paris in 1948 and then to the United States in 1952. They lived in New York, and Joanna worked for more than twenty years for the American agency of the Polish Steel Company (Stalexport) until they

---

20 Cornelia Brierly, *Tales of Taliesin: A Memoir of Fellowship*, 2nd ed. (Rohnert Park, CA: Pomegranate; Floyd Lloyd Wright Foundation, 2000), 69–70; Marya Lilien, "O Józiu Wittlinie—wspomnienia lwowskiej młodości," *Wiadomości* [London], 25 Nov. 1979, 3; Merney Rich, "Marya Lilien: Frank Lloyd Wright Opened My Mind," *Chicago Tribune*, 15 May 1988, section 6, 3; Zdzisław Żygulski Jun., "Ze Lwowa do Chicago: Wspomnienie o Marii Lilien-Czarneckiej," *Cracovia Leopolis* 2 (2005): 14–17; "Lilien, Marya de Czarnecka," in *Who's Who in Polish America: 1996–1997*, ed. Boleslaw Wierzbianski (New York: Bicentennial Pub. Corp., 1996), 262.

retired in Florida. Charles died in 1996. Joanna, despite her advanced age, is a wonderful source of knowledge and memory. It is due to Joanna's will, patience, and advice that publication of Artur Lilien's memoirs was made possible.

The English translation prepared by Marya Lilien and Joanna Grun is supplemented with their explanatory notes. These are signed with the initials M.L. and J.G. respectively. Additional annotations, prepared by author of this preface, are unsigned. The present publication indicates Polish geographical names as they were spelled by Lilien. The present-day Ukrainian names, including modern names of the streets, are mentioned in the notes at their first occurrence.

The English translation of the reminiscences and its supplements were edited and adjusted to the demands of modern publication by Yohai Goell, Jerusalem.

Publication of this book was made possible, first and foremost, thanks to Joanna Grun. I wish to express my profound gratitude to Joanna's children Catherine (Kasieńka), Ronald, and Marc Grun for their support and help. I am deeply grateful to Prof. Tom Peters for sharing with me his great knowledge of the history and genealogy of the Lilien family, and to Dr. Victoria Lunzer-Talos and Dr. Heinz Lunzer for their expertise in Joseph Roth's milieu. I am profoundly grateful to Dr. Victoria Lunzer-Talos for her insightful and thorough reading of the memoirs, for invaluable advice and queries. I wish to thank Prof. Rachel Manekin and Prof. Antony Polonsky for encouraging this publication. I am grateful to Dr. Vladimir Levin, Benjamin Lukin, Hanna Palmon, Michał Piechotka, Dr. Vita Susak, and Dr. Arkadi Zeltser for their help and advice, and to Susan Carfrae and Ilia Levin for professional photographic work.

Sergey R. Kravtsov
Jerusalem, June 2015

To Kasieńka from Grandpa

Artur Lilien-Brzozdowiecki

Artur Lilien-Brzozdowiecki, 1940s. *Courtesy of Catherine Grun*

While I am writing these words, a tempest is raging in the world. The earth trembles on its foundations. On battered boats we wrestle with stormy seas, searching for new, calmer shores. And behind us, on the vanishing horizon, old worlds are crashing to ruin.

During this tragic journey you came into this world, dear child of my child.

In your heart's blood you carry from the ruins a heritage of ages. A heritage of ancient cultures, a long line of generations of brave and noble-hearted men and women. They were leaders among their people, achieving their standing by working on perfecting themselves, as well as by their faithful and devoted service to the community; but, above all, by their deep faith that the world ought to be ruled by love.

Our part is to work, however, we are not granted to fulfill our work. Generations follow generations and are handing down unfinished tasks.

I want to leave you, my dear child, a handful of reminiscences about your predecessors, the way they live in my memory.

I want to tell you this, and that, though older things may be at times foggy, blurred, maybe even fantastic, while things more recent will be treated more broadly. About things remote in time, I want to repeat for you what I heard about them at home, though, alongside the truth, they may be part legend. About things recent, I want to tell you the way I remember and think of them.

Take it with you to these new, unknown shores, wherever you will land, so that some time you may better understand who you are yourself.

Artur Lilien-Brzozdowiecki
Cairo, Winter 1944–1945

MY GREAT-GREAT-GRANDFATHER
MAJER RACHMIEL MISES, born 1800, died 1891

He came from a family which, since time immemorial, was settled in Lwów.[1] Large tombstones of his ancestors, covered with Hebraic

---

1   Presently Lviv in Ukraine.

inscriptions, leaning with age, stood in the Old Jewish Cemetery. Their unbroken row reached back to the days of the Jagiellon dynasty.[2] His father was Fiszel,[3] his grandfather Rachmiel. A few generations earlier their name was Koziner, probably after some estate called Kozin,[4] which they might have held in lease. The given name of the wife of one of the Koziners was Mize. Next to her tomb, leaning on her husband's tomb, stands her son's gravestone. The epitaph indicates the son's relation to his father, after which it gives a matronymic byname Mises, meaning "the son of Mize."[5] Since then, this byname became accepted as the family name. Farther back, the name Koziner disappears, and the tombstones give only the given name and that of the father.[6] Thus, the stones tell the story of how the Mises originated from Koziners, and the Koziners from those Izaks, sons of Nachmans, and Nachmans, sons of Izaks, about whom a book by Majer Bałaban was published: "Jews in Lwów in the Sixteenth and Seventeenth Century."[7]

They were merchants, bankers; they held in lease the Czyżyków estate[8] near Winniki,[9] close to Lwów—they were at times collectors of Jewish taxes, and they were civic leaders. They erected the oldest synagogue of Lwów, on Blacharska (Tinsmiths) Street.[10] It was built on their commission by the same Italian master architect who built the famous Wallachian Church on nearby Ruska Street.[11]

---

2 The last of the Jagiellons died in the sixteenth century [M.L.].
3 Ephraim Fiszel Mises (d. 1842).
4 Presently Kozyn in Volhyn oblast, Ukraine.
5 Pronounced Meezeh [M.L.].
6 See Majer Bałaban, "Genealogical Tree of the Ornstein-Braude Family" (Heb.), in *Księga jubileuszowa ku czci D-ra Markusa Braudego* (Warsaw: Towarzystwo Krzewienia Nauk Judaistycznych w Polsce, 1931), 33–35; plates VIII–XI.
7 Majer Bałaban, *Żydzi lwowscy na przełomie XVIgo i XVIIgo wieku* (Lwów: Fundusz konkursowy im. H. Wawelberga, 1906).
8 Presently Chyzhykiv in Lviv oblast, Ukraine.
9 Presently Wynnyky in Lviv oblast, Ukraine.
10 Presently Fedorova Street in Lviv.
11 The architect was Paolo Romano [M.L.]. Bałaban and Lilien erred: the architect was Paulus Italus, alias Paweł Szczęśliwy, and not the builder of the Wallachian Assumption Church, whose guild nickname was Paweł Rzymianin; see Władysław Łoziński, *Sztuka lwowska w XVI i XVII wieku: Architektura i rzeźba* (Lwów: H. Altenberg, 1901), 41–42; Michał Kowalczuk, *Cech budowniczy we Lwowie za czasów polskich (do roku 1772)* (Lwów: Stow. Budowniczych, 1927), 19, 27–28.

3

In the times of Sigismund III Vasa,[12] the Jesuits began to transplant onto Polish ground the religious intolerance that was spreading all over Europe. In order to spite the Jews, they bought a lot in front of the synagogue entrance, built a house there, and forbade Jews to enter their Temple.[13] In 1580, a long, laborious lawsuit was begun by the Jewish community against the monastery; it dragged on for forty years.[14] It ended in a compromise in 1620. The agreement was brought about by the adroit policy of a matron of our family, known as Golden Rose. Even in my time, the memory of her was alive among the Lwówian Jews, and her ornate tomb was the object of a yearly pilgrimage. The agreement was highly original: the Jesuits gave the Jews their medium-size house, and the Jews in return built for the Jesuits a huge monastery.[15] It was the same building which remained standing up to World War II and stretched along most of Hetmańska Street.[16]

Around 1785, the Austrian Emperor Joseph II confiscated the monastery and it was since used as an Office of Internal Revenue.

---

12 Sigismund III Vasa (Polish: Zygmunt III Waza, 1566–1632), King of Poland and Grand Duke of Lithuania, a monarch of the united Polish-Lithuanian Commonwealth from 1587 to 1632 and king of Sweden from 1592 until he was deposed in 1599.

13 Actually, the front building was constructed by Mordechai son of Izak, who barred the Jesuits from entering the synagogue; see Bałaban, *Żydzi lwowscy*, 65–125.

14 Jesuits arrived in the city only in 1591, and the compromise was achieved in 1609; see ibid., 89–140.

15 Actually, the Jews paid a fine of 20,600 guilders; see ibid., 142. The historical Rose daughter of Yakov, a daughter-in-law of Izak son of Nachman, died in 1637. There is a legend connecting the martyrdom and death of a woman called Golden Rose— whose prototype was Rose daughter of Yakov— to the liberation of the Nachmanowicz Synagogue from Jesuit control; see ibid., 178–186. There is also a legend connecting the Golden Rose to Chmielnicki's siege of Lwów in 1648; ibid., 181.

16 Hetmańska Street presently is the eastern side of Svobody Avenue. The Office of Internal Revenue—initially the house of the Gubernial Authority—was built in 1783–1792 on the plot adjacent to the former Jesuit College, partially using the premises of the latter. The Jesuit College was built in the seventeenth century on the plot purchased at the expense of the Jewish community. After the Society of Jesus was suppressed in Austria (1773), the edifice was transformed for the needs of a court of justice and served in this capacity until 1939. The building of the Office of Internal Revenue was dismantled in 1943–1947; the building of the Jesuit College is intact.

Helena Mises, self-portrait, 1910. Canvas, oil.
Image © Borys Voznytsky National Art Gallery of Lviv

A handsome golden tankard, which belonged to Golden Rose, was in the possession of my cousin, Helenka Mises.[17] Bałaban included a picture of this tankard in his book.[18]

Helenka Mises, daughter of Emil Mises,[19] an engineer, and Matylda née Schorr,[20] was a talented painter. She married an engineer, [Max] Lurie, from Hamburg, Germany. After his death, she moved to Vienna and was lost during World War II.[21]

---

17 Helena Mises was a daughter of Emil Mises, granddaughter of Hermann Mises, and great-granddaughter of Majer Rachmiel Mises. Thus, she was Lilien's aunt, not his cousin.
18 Bałaban, *Żydzi lwowscy*, 456, fig. 76.
19 Emil Rachmiel Edler von Mises (1850–1915).
20 Matylda (Mathilde) Edle von Mises (1856–1922).
21 Helena (Helene) Lurie née Edle von Mises (1883–1942) was transported from Hamburg to Łódź and died of enteritis in the Łódź ghetto on 31 July 1942. See her biography and self-portraits in Jerzy Malinowski, *Malarstwo i rzeźba Żydów*

In Poland there was a tax called the Jewish head tax, paid by the Jews to the Royal Treasurer in return for legal protection. When, during the war with Chmielnicki,[22] King John Casimir appeared in Lwów, the Royal Treasurer called in the tax collector, our forefather Izak, son of Nachman,[23] and asked for money.

"Why, you know that the taxes have been paid for the current year."

"So, you pay for next year, and the year after. We need money for the war."

Nachmanowicz[24] therefore turned to the Jews with these words: "Better to give the king out of free will than wait till Chmielnicki comes and takes it by force." And the Jews started bringing silver and gold for advance taxes until a fair amount of money was assembled, which helped to finalize the expedition.

As a reward for this service, the king bestowed upon Nachmanowicz the former palace of the Kazanowski family, situated on the Main Square, directly opposite the main entrance to the City Hall. It was a large, four-story building, with a six-window front, two courtyards, and a passage for carriages to Boimów Street.[25] In order to understand how unique was this privilege, one has to bear in mind that no Jew was allowed to own a house outside the Jewish district at that time. The Main Square was reserved exclusively for the nobility and town patricians. The latter were allowed to own houses with a three-window front; six-window houses were a privilege of the nobility. Never before did a Jew own a house like this in Lwów.

Polskich w XIX i XX wieku (Warsaw: Wydawnictwo Naukowe PWN, 2000), 98–99; on her life in Hamburg see reminiscences by Leonardo Rosenberg: Herzenberg.net, accessed 14 December 2014, http://www.herzenberg.net/leo/htmlrh/Hamburg.html; on the circumstances of her death see the last letters from the Łódź ghetto: Jewishgen.org, accessed 14 December 2014, http://www.jewishgen.org/databases/holocaust/0194__Lodz__letters.html.

22 Chmielnicki was the leader of the Cossacks' rebellion in the then Polish Ukraine [M.L.].

23 This is an aberration of collective memory. The "forefather" Izak son of Nachman (Izak Nachmanowicz) died in 1595.

24 The ending "wicz" means "son of"—in this case: son of Nachman [M.L.].

25 Presently Staroyevreiska Street.

The Kazanowski family were magnates, but during the then recent Swedish War they sided with the king of Sweden, Carolus Gustavus.[26] This house, 18 Rynek Square,[27] was kept in my family, and in my lifetime was owned by Aunt Ewelina Klärman. Her apartment was a real museum of the most beautiful old mementos.

ے۔ ے۔ ے۔

Majer Rachmiel Mises kept a grand house in a patriarchal, old-fashioned style. His numerous sons and daughters married young, received an apartment next to him, and lived under his watchful eye. He was married to Rosa Halberstam.

He was held in general esteem. Around 1848 he was a member of a delegation from Galicia[28] to a central parliamentary body in Vienna; for many years he functioned as president of the Jewish community, and in the 1870s a hereditary nobility title was bestowed upon him by the Austrian emperor with the predicate "Edler von."[29] The family crest comprises a golden rosette in the center, in memory of the ancestress, the Golden Rose;[30] the side fields contain the book of Holy Scriptures as a symbol of knowledge and faith, and a caduceus, the symbol of commerce and leadership.

---

26 So they were considered traitors [M.L.]. This passage is not historically consistent: Carolus Gustavus, King Charles X Gustav of Sweden (1622–1660), reigned in 1654–1660; the "recent" war of 1616–1617 was waged by King Gustav Adolph. Available reference literature does not give any notice of Kazanowskis' alleged betrayal. As attested by archival sources, the discussed house was built in 1777–1785 and sold by the Armenian merchant Andrzej Andzułowski to Rachmiel Hirsz Mises on 20 August 1789 for 8,000 ducats. See Volodymyr Vuitsyk, "Ploshcha Rynok, 18," *Visnyk instytutu Ukrzakhidproektrestavratsiia* 14 (2004): 125.

27 Main Square 18 [M.L.], presently 18 Rynok Square.

28 In those times, independent Poland did not exist. It was divided between Austria, Germany, and Russia. This part was Austrian territory [M.L.].

29 Actually, Rachmiel Mises was knighted in 1881; see R. Pytel, "Mises, Majer Jerachmiel von," in *Österreichisches Biographisches Lexikon*, vol. 6 (Graz: H. Böhlau, 1975), 317.

30 In a biography of Ludwig von Mises, the coat of arms is explained in the following way: "The banner, in red, displays the Rose of Sharon, which in the litany is one of the names given to the Blessed Mother, as well as the Stars of the Royal House of David, a symbol of the Jewish people." See Jörg Guido Hülsmann, *Mises: The Last Knight of Liberalism* (Auburn: Ludwig von Mises Institute, 2007), 15.

7

Medal commemorating the ninetieth birthday of Majer Rachmiel von Mises, 1890. *Courtesy of Catherine Grun*

For his ninetieth birthday, a family medal was coined in his honor. I was able to rescue this medal when leaving home and am carrying it, wherever I go, like a talisman, and am placing here a reproduction.[31]

He believed in simplicity of style and was full of kindness. He couldn't stand ostentation. When, in his young years, he still dressed in a *bekesza*,[32] people were saying that outside it was made of plain cloth, but inside, so no one could see, it was lined in summer with most expensive silk,[33] and in winter with sable.

As far as marriages were concerned, the Mises family considered only a few other families in the country as equals. They approved of names such as Nierenstein, Halberstam, Kallir, Landau, Natanson,[34]

---

31 The cast of this medal was given to me by Artur and is still in my possession [J.G.].

32 *Bekesza* (Yiddish *bekeshe*, from Hungarian *bekes*) is a long coat, usually made of black silk. It remains a Sabbath and holiday dress of Hasidim after it went out of fashion in the nineteenth century.

33 Bałaban uses the term "the silk Jews" to characterize the well-to-do inhabitants of Sykstuska Street; see Majer Bałaban, *Historia Lwowskiej Synagogi Postępowej* (Lwów: Zarząd Synagogi Postępowej, 1937), 11.

34 The author uses a Polonized form of the surname Natansohn.

Askenazy, and Wahl. My parents met and fell in love while working for the welfare of youth. The Mises considered the Liliens inadequate and made it difficult for mother.

But the patriarch himself, Majer Rachmiel, came to her rescue; he declared that he got to know my father as a man of great heart, with a fine mind and a sense of honor; thus were the scales turned in favor of this marriage. That is how I and my children, and you, my tiny grand-daughter, we all really owe it to him that we exist on this earth.[35]

MY GREAT-GRANDFATHER
ARTUR MISES,[36] son of Majer Rachmiel

Some distant relationship connected him with the Vienna Rothschilds. They entrusted him with their affairs in Lwów and Galicia. When the Rothschild Austrian Bank of Commerce and Industry[37] opened its

---

35 Our mother, Emma Lilien née Nierenstein, was a girl with her own mind. She would have married our father with or without her family's blessings. However, when a "villain" uncle suggested that the wedding should be postponed, so great-grandfather shouldn't live to witness the "misalliance," mother was so provoked that she forced her father to go immediately to Majer R. and tell him about her engagement. On trembling feet grandfather went. Tableau! When he cautiously broke the news, the grand old man of ninety laughed, and called out: "At long last, you have come to your senses! I have known it all along, and made my inquiries. And what I hear about the young man is only the best. No, if a man that young has everyone speak of him with such love, he must have a heart, brains, and integrity." Old great-grandpa outwitted them all. With such an ally, mother was triumphant. He not only witnessed the wedding of our parents, but lived to see the fifth generation. Artur was a year old before the patriarch died [M.L.].

36 Artur (Abraham) Mises—the son of Majer Rachmiel Mises—was a brother of Hirsch Mises (1820–1887) and an uncle of Artur Edler von Mises (1854–1903),who was the father of Ludwig Heinrich von Mises (1881–1973), an Austrian economist, philosopher, author, and classical liberal who significantly influenced the modern free-market libertarian movement and the Austrian School, and Richard von Mises (1883–1953), a scientist and mathematician who worked on solid mechanics, fluid mechanics, aerodynamics, aeronautics, statistics, and probability theory. See Matthias Bergner and Karl Märker, "Mises, Edle v.," in *Neue Deutsche Biographie*, vol. 17 (Berlin: Duncker & Humblot, 1994), 563.

37 Creditanstalt [M.L.]. "K. k. privilegierte Österreichische Credit-Anstalt für Handel und Gewerbe" was founded in 1855 by Anselm Salomon Freiherr von Rothschild.

Artur Mises with his family. Photo, second half of the nineteenth century.
Courtesy of Catherine Grun

branch in Lwów, he became its first director. He was one of the initiators and board members of the first railroad in the country, which ran from Vienna via Kraków to Lwów and was named "Emperor Ferdinand Northern Railroad."

After the Polish uprising[38] came to an end in 1831, Prince Leon Sapieha[39] settled in Lwów and devoted himself to the economic development of the country. This was called at the time "Organic Work." He entered into a close relationship with Artur Mises and drew him

---

38 Against Russia [M.L.].
39 Leon Sapieha (1803–1878), a Polish nobleman, politician, and statesman.

into collaboration. Great-grandfather took an active part in the creation of institutions which endured until recently. The most important of these was "The Savings Bank of Galicia" and the "Farm and Land Credit Association." The personal relations between great-grandfather and Prince Leon were so close that his still surviving niece, our aunt Berta Kolischer, used to sit as a child in the Prince's lap.

I was named to commemorate this ancestor. His desk chair was standing at my desk in Zofiówka.[40]

∽ ∽ ∽

Great-grandfather was related to the Bernsteins. Ignacy Bernstein was referred to as "uncle" in our home.[41] He was a noted collector of works containing proverbs of various epochs and nations. This specialized library contained tens of thousands of volumes, and the thick catalog alone was of bibliographic interest. He himself collected and published an ample volume of Jewish proverbs and gave me a copy,[42] reciprocating for an ancient edition of proverbs by Erasmus of Rotterdam which I had sent him as a gift. It seems to me that this library somehow came to Brussels.

Berta, the daughter of great-grandpa's sister[43] and sister of Aunt Ewelina Klärman,[44] married Dr. Henryk Kolischer, a man of great knowledge and great fortune.[45] He was a congressman in the Vienna parliament for many terms, then a member of the Polish Sejm,[46] and

---

40 Pronounced Zofiufka [M.L.]. Presently Sofiivka, a neighborhood bounded by Stry-iska, Panasa Myrnoho, Yaroslavenka, Dibrovna, and Sventsytskoho streets.

41 Ignacy Bernstein (1836, Vinnytsia–1909, Brussels) was married to Eliza (Elise), daughter of Majer Rachmiel Mises. See Herman Rosenthal, "Bernstein, Ignacy," in *The Jewish Encyclopedia*, vol. 3 (New York: Funk & Wagnalls, 1903), 100.

42 Ignatz Bernstein, *Yiddish Proverbs and Idioms* (Yiddish), 2nd ed. (Warsaw: Kaufman, 1908).

43 Berta (Bertha) Celina Klärman (1862–?), daughter of Samuel Klärman and Ernes-tina (Esther), née Mises.

44 Eliza Ewelina Klärman (1866–?).

45 Dr. Henryk Kolischer (1853–1932) was a businessman, a member of the Sejm of Galicia in 1901–1913 and of the Legislative Sejm of the Second Polish Republic in 1919–1922, president of the Chamber of Commerce in Lwów (1927). Kolischer was educated as a physician, lawyer, and agronomist.

46 Parliament [M.L.].

finally, the president of the Chamber of Commerce and Industry in Lwów. Aunt Berta moved in the best circles of European society all her life. In her Vienna palace on Reisnerstrasse, I used to meet such people as Princess Pauline Metternich,[47] wife of the late Austrian ambassador to the court of Napoleon III, or the famous Austrian foreign minister, Count Berchtold.[48] She was very beautiful and very distinguished; until her old age she maintained her naïve charm. She was always deeply involved in the life of her fellow humans and did much to help people. She was a very close friend of my mother.

Tragedy befell her in her old age: her son was murdered by the Nazis in Otwock.[49] Her daughter[50] together with her husband Marjan Reich managed to make it to New York with Berta and Ewelina; there, she was lured to some hotel, where she was murdered and robbed of her jewels.[51] The son-in-law grabbed what was saved from the war of their immense fortune, and handed out to Aunt Berta only the mere necessities of daily life. Thus, the orphaned old lady, in her eighties, now lives with her sister and an aged servant in some little New York hotel while my sisters and I send her some modest help.

MY GREAT-GRANDMOTHER
JOANNA HALBERSTAM, wife of Artur Mises

She was the beloved grandmother of my mother. Mama lost her mother when she was a little over ten. Her grandmother Joanna then took over the guidance of her education. In my family portrait collection in Zofiówka I had her portrait, painted by Maurycy Gottlieb, the famous pupil of Matejko.[52] Frequently gazing at this canvass, I found

---

47 Pauline Metternich (1836–1921).
48 Leopold Berchtold (1863–1942), an Austro-Hungarian politician.
49 A sanatorium [M.L.]. Maurycy Marceli Kolischer (1894–1942).
50 Zuzanna Flora Kolischer (1889–?).
51 In 1942.
52 Maurycy Gottlieb (1856–1879), a Jewish Polish painter; Jan Matejko (1838–1892), an outstanding Polish painter.

Joanna Mises née Halberstam. Portrait by Leonhard(?) Bülow.
Courtesy of Catherine Grun

a great resemblance to my mother. Not only were the features alike, but there was a similar countenance and austerity, along with goodness and intellect. In my imagination she was an authoritarian embodying some ancient matriarchal traditions, so much alive in my mother too.

Mother owned a portrait collection of progenitresses on the distaff side, which she then gave to her oldest daughter, my sister Klara, who is married in America. The first is Bella Halberstam née Herzenstein; after her Joanna Mises née Halberstam; then Klara Nierenstein née Mises, and Emma Lilien née Nierenstein. Klara Bloomfield née Lilien

13

Bella Halberstam née Herzenstein. Miniature portrait, mid-nineteenth century. *Courtesy of Catherine Grun*

received them [the portraits], and after her probably her daughter Margit will have them.[53]

There is something in the idea of the matriarchy that often intrigued me. Truly, the mother is more important than the father in handing down to her children the cultural achievements of former generations. She has more contact with them and influences them more directly. The sense of respect for the woman and for the mother was highly instilled in us.

---

53 Margie was not interested, so I, Marya Lilien-Czarnecka, took most of these portrait-miniatures [M.L.].

There were many bankers and rabbis in great-grandmother's family. Her father, Wolf Halberstam, lived in the "Free City of Brody"[54] with another great-grandfather of mine, Mendel Nierenstein, who ran a sizeable bank called "Halberstam & Nierenstein."

Great-grandma's mother was Bella Halberstam née Herzenstein. She came from Szarogród in Ukraine.[55] Her father was a rich man there, known as "der Szarogroder Ruff."[56] During one of the Russian-Turkish wars, he founded a military hospital at his own expense.[57] He was the first Jew who ever received a title of Russian nobility. There exists an old copper engraving showing the scene of the Tsar presenting him with a diamond ring.[58]

In Szarogród there was a castle of a Polish magnate family. Great-grandmother Bella received her education there, together with

---

54 Presently Brody in Lviv oblast, Ukraine. The status of a "Free City" meant a tax-free trade zone on the Austrian-Russian border.

55 Presently Sharhorod in Vinnytsia oblast, Ukraine. Szarogród was founded by Great Chancellor Jan Zamoyski in 1585 and named after his coat of arms—Szary. At the turn of the eighteenth century, Szarogród belonged to the Lubomirski aristocratic family.

56 The word "Ruff" here stands for "ruv" (*rav*, rabbi) in local Yiddish pronunciation.

57 David Herzenstein, the rabbi of Szarogród and a first-guild merchant, was acknowledged by Emperor Paul I (reigned 1796–1801) in May 1798 and awarded a golden medal in February 1799 for his benevolent activity that hindered a plague epidemic in 1797–1798. Herzenstein was the first Jew to be awarded a Russian medal. See Dmitrii Feldman and Dmitrii Peters, *Istoriia nagrazhdeniia rossiiskikh evreev za voennye i grazhdanskie zaslugi v nachale XIX veka* (Moscow: Drevlekhranilishche, 2006), 22–37; Dmitrii Feldman, *Rossiiskie evrei v epokhu napoleonovskikh voin* (Moscow: Drevlekhranilishche, 2013), 18–43. Herzenstein donated wheat flour to the Russian army during the Russo-Turkish war of 1806–1812 and was awarded a "present": see ibid., 28–29; Mikhail Grinberg, Benjamin Lukin, and Ilia Lurie, eds., *1812 god: Rossia i evrei. Russko-evreiskie istochniki o voine 1812 goda* (Moscow: Gesharim, 2012), 93. Herzenstein was recommended for the "deputation of Jewish people" as a first-guild merchant in 1817, see Feldman, *Rossiiskie evrei*, 29.

58 Lilien's information is not accurate; David Herzenstein had never been ennobled. He was, however, declared an honorary and hereditary citizen of Odessa in 1837; Russian State Historical Archives in St. Petersburg, collection 1343, inventory 39, file 1046. I am grateful to Benjamin Lukin for bringing this document to my attention.

the daughter of the house, in an atmosphere of high culture.[59] Later, she did much traveling and loved fine furniture. I still had in Zofiówka a bombée front decorative small armoire, which she once brought from Paris.

I also owned an old edition of Racine, which her brother once gave to his niece (my great-grandmother Joanna) for her birthday, in which he placed the following inscription:

Cadeau fait au jour de naissance à Mlle Jeanne Halberstam par son oncle et fidèle ami,

Léon de Herzenstein
Odessa, 1831[60]

Exactly a hundred years later, I gave this book to my little daughter,[61] your mama, for her birthday, as she bears the name of this great-grandmother Joanna, and I added a second inscription:

Cadeau fait au jour de naissance à l'arrière-arrière petite fille de la susdite, Mlle Jeanne Lilien-Brzozdowiecka, par son père et fidèle ami, Artur Lilien-Brzozdowiecki

Lwów, 1931[62]

When my parents went to Crimea on their honeymoon, they stopped in Odessa on the way to visit with the Halberstams, who were still living there.

One member of the Herzenstein family was a noted deputy of the Duma,[63] representing the Constitutional Democratic Party. He was murdered by the "Black Hundred."

---

59 According to my mother, Bella was a linguist who spoke Italian, French, and English, and also was a fine pianist [M.L.].
60 A birthday gift to Ms. Joanna Halberstam from her uncle and faithful friend, Leon Herzenstein, Odessa, 1831.
61 This book was in my father's library, together with all the other books, when the Russians took Zofiówka in 1939 [J.G.].
62 A birthday gift to a great-great granddaughter of the aforementioned, Ms. Joanna Lilien-Brzozdowiecka, from her father and faithful friend, Artur Lilien-Brzozdowiecki Lwów, 1931.
63 The Russian parliament [M.L.]. Mikhail Yakovlevich Herzenstein (1859–14 July 1906).

Klara Nierenstein née Mises, 1869. Courtesy of Catherine Grun

MY GRANDMOTHER
KLARA NIERENSTEIN née Mises, daughter of Artur[64]

She left several portraits painted by outstanding artists. A beautiful oval face, framed in rich dark hair, looks from these canvasses. One feels a breeze of sweet gentleness, tenderness, and subtlety from the Biedermeier times.[65]

---

64 Klara Nierenstein (1843–1879).
65 The Biedermeier times refer to the period between the Congress of Vienna (1815) and the European revolutions of 1848. Biedermeier denotes a middle-class Neo-Classicist style, often marked by some sweetness and sentimentality, in literature and art. Klara's known photograph dates 1869, much later than the conventional Biedermeier times.

She was highly educated. They said that she was a living dictionary of German, French, English, and Italian. I read the old yellowed pages of letters which she, as a very young girl, wrote to her parents in Karlsbad. Charming descriptions of smart gentlemen in tight trousers with leather straps, as they ambled through the Jesuit Garden[66] accompanied by ladies in crinolines.

In 1863 she translated and published in Polish Macaulay's treatise "About Jews."[67]

She died very young,[68] leaving three orphaned children. My mother was the oldest. [69] Then there was Uncle Emil[70] and Aunt Ella.[71]

Her husband, grandfather Nierenstein, survived her by some scores of years and till the end of his life he mourned for her. In his bedroom, on an easel, stood the best of her portraits by the Viennese artist Angeli.[72] It was always covered by a dark curtain, which grandfather often lifted when he was alone in his room and then spent a long time pondering and looking.

Aunt Ella married Dr. Maurice Weinreb, a gynecologist, who settled in Berlin. In her old age she became mentally ill and died in a sanatorium. Her daughter, "little Klarusia," called thus to distinguish her from my sister, was an assistant professor of chemistry at the University of Berlin. During the Hitler expulsions, she returned to Lwów, where they owned a house. When in 1939 the Soviets occupied Lwów, she volunteered, presuming that she would be assigned work according to her high skills. They gave her work—shoveling snow at the railroad

---

66 A public park in Lwów [M.L.]. Today the park is named after Ivan Franko.
67 Thomas Babington Macaulay (1800–1859), a British historian and Whig politician. Thomas B. Macaulay, *O Żydach*, trans. K . . .y M. (Lwów: E. Winiarz, 1863). The translated work is idem, "Statement of the Civil Disabilities and Privations affecting Jews in England," *Edinburgh Review* (January 1831): 363–374.
68 Klara Nierenstein died in 1879 in the thirty-sixth year of her life.
69 Emma Cecylia (Cicilie) Nierenstein (1867–1934).
70 Emil Heinrich Nierenstein (1866–1906). According to the birth records, Emil was the elder brother. See Lviv PSA AGAD Births 1866, no. 49. Rudolf Wilhelm Nierenstein, not mentioned by Artur Lilien, was born after Emil Heinrich, in October 1872. See Lviv PSA AGAD Births 1872–1873, no. 23.
71 Rafaela Rebeka Nierenstein (b. 1876). See Lviv PSA AGAD Births 1876, no. 68.
72 Heinrich von Angeli (1840–1925).

station.[73] Aunt Ella's son is an engineer; in time, he left Berlin for London.[74]

I never knew Uncle Emil, he died young.[75] But my mother often spoke about him. He was a very gifted child. As a young man he studied Sanskrit and was deeply involved in yoga knowledge, practiced fasts[76] and Buddhist rites.

My mother wasn't unaffected by his influence. I remember how she once tried to explain to me the meaning of the Indian word "karma," and repeatedly quoted the teachings, how the acts of a human being shape the contents of his soul.

HERMAN MISES, brother of grandmother Klara

He was well-educated, with a brilliant mind. He devoted himself to politics and around 1874 was elected in Drohobycz as a member of the Vienna parliament.[77]

He became a member of the "Polish Circle." In his speeches and writings he launched the idea that an alliance on a world-wide scale should be created between the Polish nation and the Jews. As they are both ill-treated, they could contribute much to each other: the Poles, by supporting everywhere Jewish pursuits for emancipation, and the Jews, by supporting with their influence throughout the world the cause of Polish independence. He published a magazine in Vienna, entitled—I think—*East and West*.[78]

---

73 Unfortunately, little Klarusia disappeared during the subsequent Nazi occupation; probably killed in a concentration camp [M.L.]

74 Henryk Emmanuel Weinreb Wyndham (1905–1977).

75 Emil Heinrich Nierenstein died in 1906; see online archives of the Jewish Community Hospital (Foundation of Maurycy Lazarus), see Dcjr.org, accessed 12 June 2015, http://www.dcjr.org/index.php/non-vital-records/hospital-records/ 1829-nirenstein-emil-henryk. He studied at polytechnic universities of Lwów and Vienna (1888–1889). *Księga Pamiątkowa Towarzystwa "Bratniej Pomocy" Słuchaczów Politechniki we Lwowie* (Lwów: Tow. "Bratniej Pomocy" Słuchaczów Politechniki: 1897), 248.

76 He was a vegetarian [M.L.].

77 Herman von Mises (1836–1910) was elected to the Imperial Council (Reichsrat) of the fifth convocation, in 1873–1879.

78 Herman von Mises (1836–1910) edited the *Wiener Allgemeine Zeitung*. See J. Zdrada, "Mises Herman von, publizist und politiker," in *Österreichisches Biographisches Lexikon* 6 (Graz: H. Böhlau, 1975), 317.

He lived to an old age, and lost his money when old. My father took care of him. The old gentleman moved to our house on Sykstuska Street[79] and ate with us. He always read many difficult books and liked to encourage me in discussions—and I was very fond of him. It pleased me to listen to his long tales of parliament days, of historic events in which he took a part, like the Congress of Berlin in 1878, or of people he met and knew, like Disraeli,[80] Bismarck,[81] Andrássy,[82] and Gorchakov;[83] of scientific questions; of politics and economy. I learned much from these talks and I owe much to him.

I think that I resemble him somewhat in features as well as in temperament. There is also a resemblance in me of his father, my great-grandfather Artur.

MY GRANDFATHER

MAURYCY NIERENSTEIN, b. 1840, d. 1917, husband of Klara Mises

He came from one of those Jewish families who, during the Crusades, fled from the Rhineland to Poland and bore names of towns as their surnames (Landau, Oppenheim, Mannheimer, Katzenellenbogen, etc.). In Poland, the Nierensteins acquired substantial wealth centuries ago and enjoyed a high standing. Under the Austrian annexation, they were called "The Jewish Schwarzenbergs."[84] The generations I remembered in

---

79 Presently Doroshenka Street.
80 Benjamin Disraeli (1804–1881), a British Conservative politician of Jewish origin, prime minister under Queen Victoria.
81 Otto von Bismarck (1815–1898), a German statesman, the main "architect" of the German Empire ("Kaiserreich").
82 Gyula Andrássy (1823–1890), a Hungarian statesman, prime minister after the division of the Austro-Hungarian monarchy into Austrian and Hungarian states, a promoter of Hungarian interests.
83 Alexander Mikhailovich Gorchakov (1798–1883), a Russian statesman, foreign minister, and a chancellor of the Russian Empire.
84 Schwarzenberg, a Bohemian and Franconian aristocratic family. Since the seventeenth century they rallied with the Habsburg Emperors in Vienna and developed as one of the most important princely families, providing statesmen and military leaders.

Ozjasz Nierenstein, miniature portrait by Nowak (Odessa), first half of the nineteenth century. Władysław Bachowski and Mieczysław Treter, Wystawa miniatur i sylwetek we Lwowie 1912 (Lwów, 1912), VIII–57.
Courtesy of Borys Voznytsky National Art Gallery of Lviv

my lifetime were settled in Brody.[85] After the abolition of the tax privileges of the "Free City,"[86] they moved to Lwów, and some to Vienna.

Maurycy's grandfather, Mendel, was the banker of Brody (Halberstam & Nierenstein). His son, my great-grandfather Ozjasz Nierenstein, settled in Lwów.

I don't know exactly what part he took in political life. Prince Leon Sapieha mentions him in his memoirs. He writes that when he once took an uncompromising stand for the Polish cause in the Vienna parliament against the Austrian court, the other Polish delegates were

---

85 Brody, a town northeast of Lwów, was a tax-free center for trade with Russia, Turkey, and the Middle East [M.L.]. It was also an important Jewish religious and cultural center.
86 Brody benefited from its tax privileges in 1779–1880.

21

uneasy and began avoiding him. Some even stopped greeting him on the streets. Only "Lubomirski and a banker from Lwów, Nierenstein" did not change their old cordial relation to the prince.

When the limitations upon Jews to own property beyond the ghetto were lifted, my great-grandfather acquired the stately main post office building. And so, the Nierensteins settled in the showy building at 23 Sykstuska Street, generally known as "The Old Post Office." Later, grandfather Maurycy lived there. Still later, my parents took an apartment there, and always stayed there during the winter. The summers were spent in Zofiówka. So did I live this way throughout my childhood.

The neo-classic white front was lovely, the masonry walls very thick, there was a vast staircase and tremendous rooms. Our apartment was once the dwelling of "Mister President."[87] In two salons there were

Sykstuska Street, view toward the west. Postcard, 1917. *Courtesy of the Urban Media Archives, Center for Urban History of East Central Europe, Lviv*

---

87 This probably refers to Aleksander Jasiński (1823–1897), who officiated as the first president of Lwów City in 1873–1880.

precious floors of artful and intricate marquetry designs in diverse woods. I saw similar floors only in the Royal Castle in Warsaw.

Grandfather Nierenstein's mother was born Wahl. Her portraits show a completely different type than other family portraits—peaceful and poised. Hers show lively eyes, an aquiline nose, activity, and curiosity.

The Wahls came to Poland during the reign of Sigismund Augustus.[88] While the Nierensteins were Ashkenazi Jews, the Wahls were Sephardim.

Prince Radziwiłł "Sierotka"[89] met in Padua a physician: Saul, the son of Rabbi Maharam Padua,[90] and took him to Poland, to his castle in Nieśwież. The prince trusted him greatly. Saul soon was not only the prince's doctor but also his confidant and counselor. In time, his role grew to a kind of state minister at the almost sovereign Radziwiłł's court.

There is a legend among the Jews that during the first free elections,[91] it was suspected that one of the political parties might forcefully take possession of the crown jewels for the Valois or the Habsburgs, and as they looked for a secure place to hide them, Saul was entrusted with them. Therefore, said the Jews, he was for one night the Polish king. Hence also comes his byname Wahl (meaning: election), which became the family name.

His father, Rabbi Maharam Padua, pleased with the son's career, published in his honor a book in Hebrew which I saw in the possession of an attorney in Lwów, Dr. Wahl. The book is entitled *Gdola Saul*,[92] i.e., "The Greatness of Saul." A great part of the introduction is taken up by genealogic treatises, leading back to King David, as was customary with rabbis of that time. In this way they tried to reserve for their descendants the possibility of producing the Messiah.

---

88 Sigismund Augustus, the last of the Jagiellons, ruled from 1548 to 1572 [M.L.].

89 Mikołaj Krzysztof Radziwiłł "Sierotka" (1549–1616).

90 Rabbi Meir ben Isaac Katzenellenbogen of Padua (known by the Hebrew acronym, the Maharam of Padua, 1482–1565).

91 The first dynasty was the Piast; the second the Jagiellonian. After that, kings were elected by national vote of the nobility [M.L.].

92 Tzvi-Hirsh Edelman, *Gdulat Shaul* (London, 1854). The book is a compilation of earlier publications and manuscripts.

Historians rejected those distant deductions as fantasy, but they accepted as authentic the stories that occurred several centuries earlier than the time they were written. This authentic part is highly interesting.

Toward the end of the fifteenth century, the family fled to Livorno, seeking shelter from the persecution of the Spanish Inquisition. Later, they settled in Padua. Previously, on the Iberian Peninsula, their fates varied. They played a major role at the court of the caliphs of Cordova, where their presence can be traced back to the eleventh century.

It is possible that there is some connection with the Jewish state minister at the [court of the] Moors, Hasdai ibn Shaprut,[93] who in the early tenth century tried [to create] relations with the Jewish Khazar government. The capital of that country was located in Astrakhan, and its frontiers reached up to Białowieża, called by them Sar-Kil. I heard that Modelski wrote about it (*Letters of King Gebalim*).[94]

Byzantium, for obvious reasons, tried to hinder Hasdai's contacts. It wanted to prevent an understanding between the hostile Muslim world and the powerful enemies in the North. King Gebalim wrote to Hasdai to Cordova: "Do not send letters by way of Byzantium. Send them either through the south, the country of the Bulgarians, or through the west, the country 'Nemet.'"

This way, through this great-grandmother, we came in for a share of blood from distant Sephardic-Moorish worlds, maybe even with some Negroid admixture. Through the Halberstams and Herzensteins we inherited Khazar blood, probably not without a Mongolian admixture. The Nierensteins brought, comparatively, the purest Semitic blood. The Mises probably had much Slavic blood, from the times when Jewish proselytism was spreading, before the country accepted Christianity. (Nestor mentions Jewish apostles in Kiev.)[95] The Germanic and probably Latin elements of the Lilien lineage will be mentioned later.

---

93 Hasdai (Abu Yusuf ben Yitzhak ben Ezra) ibn Shaprut, ca. 915–970 or 990.
94 Teofil Emil Modelski, *Król "Gebalim" w liście Chasdaja: studyum historyczne z X w.* (Lwów: Towarzystwo dla Popierania Nauki Polskiej, 1910).
95 Nestor, the first chronicler of Russia, at that time: Ruthenia [Rus' —S. K.], [M. L.].

Jews lived in Poland as early as pagan times. Around 900 CE, an Arab traveler, Ibn Jakob,[96] crossed Poland from end to end, going to the Baltic Sea for amber. He left the oldest description of the Polish territories, and mentions Jewish farm settlements therein. Some of them were Khazars, who wandered in from the East, and some were Slavs who converted to Judaism.

During Jewish massacres by Crusaders in Western Europe, a wave of refugees from the West rushed in; they found here [in Poland] local Jews of Slavic descent and others of Turano-Mongolian blood. Later, when religious segregation came, they all had to live together in ghettos. There they integrated in the course of centuries and merged to a new neo-Judaic race.

In the eyes of his family, grandpa Nierenstein was eccentric. They expected that he, like all the others, would go into business and public affairs. But his interests took a different turn. He was only a "grand seigneur" who traveled much and loved art. Since his early youth he started painting, and was a pupil of Franciszek Tepa.[97] He brought precious souvenirs from his trips and wrote reports on monuments and art collections. His own collections kept growing, and collecting became his most important passion. His apartment was gradually changing into a museum, overloaded with paintings, porcelain, crystal, and bronzes. The best was his collection of miniatures, among them Isabey,[98] Daffinger,[99] Theer[100] and other celebrities. Treter[101] once arranged an extensive exhibition in Lwów of miniatures from private collections. An illustrated

---

96 Abraham ben Jacob, better known under his Arabic name of Ibrâhîm ibn Ya`qûb, was a tenth-century Hispano-Arab, plausibly a Sephardi Jewish traveler.
97 Franciszek Tepa (1829–1889), a painter of portraits and popular subjects, one of the first Polish artists who depicted Egypt and the Holy Land.
98 Jean Baptiste Isabey (1767–1855), a French painter of portraits and miniatures for the elite.
99 Moritz Michael Daffinger (1790–1849), an Austrian painter of miniatures.
100 The brothers Robert Theer (1818–1863), Adolf Theer (1811–1868), and Albert Theer (1815–1902), Austrian painters of miniatures. Nierenstein owned a portrait of Moritz Daffinger by Albert Theer; see Władysław Bachowski and Mieczysław Treter, *Wystawa miniatur i sylwetek we Lwowie 1912* (Lwów: Komitet Wystawy: Gubrynowicz i Syn, 1912), no. 558.
101 Mieczysław Treter (1883–1943), an art historian and theorist.

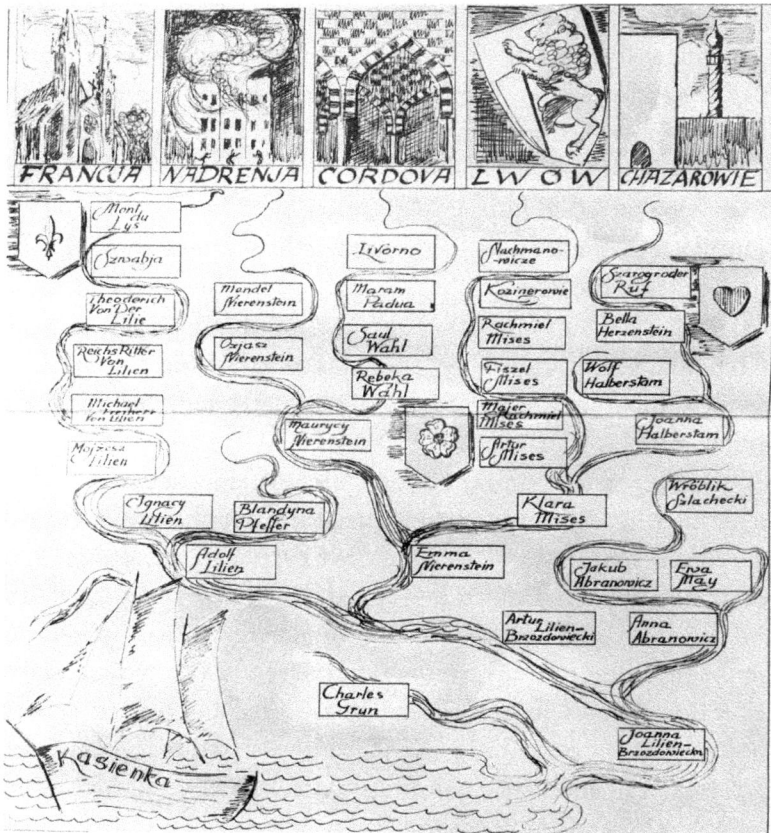

**Ancestors of Kasieńka. Genealogical tree,
drawing by Marya Lilien-Czarnecka.** *Courtesy of Catherine Grun*

catalog was published, wherein grandfather's collection is adequately represented.[102]

Grandfather's greatest pride was a portrait of Saskia, which he considered to be an original by Rembrandt.[103] His grandfather Mendel had purchased the painting from one of Napoleon's soldiers, who in 1813 was returning from the Moscow expedition through Brody and had the painting wrapped in rags and tied to the shaft of his horse-sleigh.

---

102 The exhibition catalog listed nineteen miniatures from Maurycy Nierenstein's collection; see Bachowski and Treter, *Wystawa miniatur*, 233.

103 Rembrandt Harmenszoon van Rijn (1606–1669), a Dutch artist. Saskia van Uylenburgh was his wife.

Maurycy Nierenstein, watercolor by Franciszek Tepa.
Image © Borys Voznytsky National Art Gallery of Lviv

But when the canvas was sent a hundred years later for an expert opinion to Prof. Bode in Berlin,[104] his verdict was that it was only a very fine old copy, probably painted by one of the master's pupils under his supervision. This, however, did not stop grandfather from considering the canvas his "Family Rembrandt."

In his old age, Grandfather was becoming more and more eccentric, and endless anecdotes about him were circulated. Once a week he used to travel to Żółkiew[105] to inspect his glass factory. It was managed by directors who systematically cheated Grandfather and got rich. He in turn had to throw into the bargain considerable sums year after year. But in return, his designs and artistic ideas were executed there, and he rejoiced like a child, bringing back objects

---

104 Wilhelm von Bode (1845–1929), a German art historian and curator, creator of the Kaiser Friedrich Museum (today the Bode Museum) in Berlin.
105 Presently Zhovkva in Lviv oblast, Ukraine.

made of glass and of his invention. An inkwell, which could stand on four sides, so the ink would be freed of sediment (it bore the name "Konfederatka"),[106] a double vodka glass with two containers fused together bottom to bottom ("wypij zdrów, nalej znów"),[107] or pretty cut-glass vases and flacons, on which the fancy work cost several times their value.

Some medieval rabbi, Grandfather's ancestor, as was the custom of rabbis of that time, left to posterity his genealogy back to King David. Grandfather took these deductions seriously and had his calling cards printed with this file of ancestors. This curiosity was reproduced in Maksymilian Goldstein's book on Polish Jews.[108]

Once Grandfather obtained an audience with the Pope, and he used to tell, not without pride, how he received the papal benediction for himself and his family.

Grandfather had an old faithful servant, Wilhelm Lind. He was ever-present; he went with him on travels and knew all his habits and whims. When, after grandfather's death, his apartment remained unoc-cupied and intact for many years, Wilhelm came to clean it every day: he dusted it and—like Gerwazy in *Pan Tadeusz*[109]—he wound all the clocks, useful to nobody.

Several good portraits of grandfather remained. Two were in my possession: an excellent watercolor by Franciszek Tepa from 1885, showing in profile his elongated, very noble features, and a good oil portrait, full face, in a soft hat, by our cousin Helenka Mises.

Distinguished historian Szymon Askenazy was related to the Nierensteins. He was the teacher of a whole pleiad of young Polish

---

106 *Konfederatka* is the Polish generic name for an asymmetrical, peaked, four-pointed cap used by various Polish military units throughout the ages.
107 "Cheers and fill again."
108 The calling card reads (in Hebrew, translated by Maksymilian Goldstein into Polish): "Meir son of Joseph Joshua Nierenstein of the family of men famous in Israel, Ḥakham Tzvi Ashkenazi and Meir Katzenellenbogen, rabbi in Padua, of Isaiah's breed, King David's house;" see Maksymilian Goldstein and Karol Dresdner, *Kultura i sztuka ludu żydowskiego na ziemiach polskich: zbiory Maksy-miliana Goldsteina* (Lwów: M. Goldstein, 1935), 8.
109 *Pan Tadeusz* is an epic poem by Polish poet Adam Mickiewicz, first published in 1834.

Maurycy Nierenstein, 1914. Courtesy of Catherine Grun

historians. He wrote a number of outstanding works, like *Prince Joseph Poniatowski*,[110] *Napoleon and Poland*,[111] *Gdansk and Poland*,[112] and more.

---

110 Szymon Askenazy, *Książę Józef Poniatowski 1763–1813* (Warsaw: Gebethner i Wolff, 1905).

111 Szymon Askenazy, *Napoleon a Polska*, 2 vols. (Warsaw: Towarzystwo Wydawnicze, 1918).

112 Szymon Askenazy, *Gdańsk a Polska* (Warsaw: Gebethner i Wolff, 1919).

For several years he was Poland's representative at the League of Nations in Geneva. When in Lwów, he always used to pay us a visit.

MY MOTHER

EMMA LILIEN née Nierenstein, daughter of Maurycy and Klara née Mises, 1867–1934

In her early childhood, my mother lost her mother. Since then, her education was guided by her grandmother Joanna. She was surrounded by a swarm of bonnes,[113] governesses, and teachers, whom she later always remembered with warm feelings. Miss Kanner, who later settled in America, sometimes came back to see mother. Sometimes an old mathematician, Prof. Fąfara, came to see her. I remember him from my childhood; he had a house in Żelazna Woda,[114] near our Zofiówka. Among the school subjects, mother was most interested in languages, literature, natural history, and social science. She thoroughly studied Buckle,[115] Taine,[116] Carlyle,[117] and Darwin.[118] However, she didn't neglect physical culture and sports. She was a good swimmer, and told us with pleasure how she once passed "the great test" in the Army Swimming Establishment on Pełczyński Pond.

When she grew up, composed and poised, though filled with interests, she was most of all concerned about duties toward human society. The issue of equal rights for women was in the air all around at that time and mother became one of the first pioneers of this movement on the Lwowian ground.[119] An important postulate was the struggle to admit women into higher studies. Some university professors supported

---

113 Bonnes (Fr.), meaning, nursemaids.
114 Presently Zalizna Voda, meaning, "Iron Water."
115 Henry Thomas Buckle (1821–1862), an English philosopher and historian.
116 Hippolyte Adolphe Taine (1828–1893), a French critic and historian.
117 Thomas Carlyle (1795–1881), a Scottish philosopher, satirical writer, essayist, and historian.
118 Charles Robert Darwin (1809–1882), an English naturalist who established the theory of evolution.
119 Lwów was the capital of "Austrian Poland," called at that time Galicia [M.L.].

this demand. Taking advantage of academic autonomy, they at first allowed only a few girls to attend their lectures as auditors. Mother belonged to the first such group at the University of Lwów. She attended zoology lectures given by the old "Siberian," Prof. Dybowski.[120]

These experiences created a warm friendship between her and Henryka Pawlewska,[121] a cousin of the famous Skłodowska-Curie.[122] Ève Curie[123] quotes in her book[124] numerous letters, "Lettres à Henriette," written by Mme. Curie to just this Mrs. Pawlewska. With Skłodowska herself, mother was closely acquainted. She used to tell us how she went to see her once in Paris. Skłodowska was a poor student, and mother found her scrubbing the floor of her tiny room, located on the eighth floor. Skłodowska explained to mother her theory that such gymnastics allow a tired mind to relax.[125]

In the sphere of social work she met and fell in love with my father. With determination and stubbornness, she had to force through her family's consent to this marriage.

Early photos of Mama show an austere and earnest type of beauty. Thick brows, almost grown together over thoughtful eyes, a narrow straight nose and lips, thick dark hair contrasting with light steel-blue eyes. There were daguerreotypes from her childhood in a Scotch plaid skirt, and there were lovely photos from her maiden days; there was a

---

120 After the uprising in 1863, many Polish fighters were deported by the Russians to Siberia. Those who returned were highly respected by their fellow Poles [M.L.]. Benedykt Dybowski (1833–1930), a Polish naturalist, traveler, and explorer.

121 Henryka Pawlewska, née Michałowska (1860–?), a social activist, wife of the rector of the Lwów Polytechnic School, Bronisław Pawlewski.

122 Maria Skłodowska-Curie (1867–1934), the first woman to win a Nobel Prize.

123 Ève Denise Curie Labouisse (1904–2007), a French-American writer, journalist, and pianist of Polish descent. Ève Curie was the younger daughter of Marie Skłodowska-Curie and Pierre Curie.

124 Probably: Ève Denise Curie, *Madame Curie: A Biography*, trans. Vincent Sheean (Garden City, NY: Doubleday, Doran and Co., 1938).

125 Among other activities, mother was the president for Galicia of the International League for the Protection of Women. At an international convention in London, mother met and made friends with a collaborator and friend of the famous Jane Addams from Chicago (founder of Hull House). She invited her to Lwów and I remember her as our house guest. (I don't remember her name, but it might have been Miss Smith.) [M.L.].

portrait painted by Grandfather, showing her in a brown dress closed up to her chin, full of a Grottgeresque mood.[126]

The wedding took place on 19 May 1889. I came into this world the next year.

In winter we lived at Sykstuska Street, in summer—in beloved Zofiówka. This house was built by grandfather Lilien as a summer residence for himself and his sons. Through the several summer months, the whole family assembled there for "fresh air," and the multiplying cluster of grandchildren skipped around the garden, the grove, and the fields.

The house was run on a large scale, with a lot of travels and many guests; there were parties and house concerts; on the walls good paintings continued to be added. Three years after me, Klara was born, and seven years after her, Mania.[127]

Family life did not keep mother from her social work. In my memories I always see her busy with meetings, committees, organizing lectures, day nurseries, summer colonies for poor children, etc.[128] Her most lively interest was the cause of the protection of women and the fight against white slave traffic. She went to congresses in different European capitals. On one such occasion she witnessed an unusual scene. At a reception at the home of the London Rothschilds, a black Jewish skullcap was placed at every man's table cover. Before sitting down, all—Jews and non-Jews—even the English state ministers present, donned the skullcaps, and Britain's Chief Rabbi recited the blessing for the meal. Only then did they take off the caps and began to eat.

Mother was always surrounded by numerous elderly spinsters, helpers, and secretaries, who, along with numerous guests, sat with us at the table.

---

126 Grottger was an outstanding Polish painter living in Lwów [M.L.]. Artur Grottger (1837–1867), a Polish Romantic painter and graphic artist.

127 Klara Bloomfield née Lilien (1893–1965). Mania is a Polish endearing form of Marya, Maria.

128 She really enjoyed the company of children, and often repeated that children are much more interesting than grown-ups: "They always say original things, and how many grown people are original? You mostly know what they will say next; with a child, you never know." Mother therefore also liked the company of artists, and she considered them the highest class of society. So children and artists alike adored mother [M.L.].

Through her activities, mother formed a friendship with Miss Bertha Pappenheim of Frankfurt, with whom she even discovered some ancient blood ties.[129] Miss Pappenheim published and dedicated to mother memoirs of her ancestress, Glückel von Hameln, a Jewish matron from the time of the Thirty Years' War.[130] The stormy life of that woman, brought up to have a quiet family life, found so many analogies in our times.

As Miss Pappenheim's secretary, a certain Martha Baer sometimes came with her to Lwów.[131] She had a deep voice and some hair on her face. After some years she discovered that she was really a man, changed the pace of life, donned men's clothes, and wrote a book, *Aus eines Mannes Mädchenjahren*.[132]

My father died when he was only 47 years old. Mother took over the pursuit of affairs in her hands and with great firmness guarded her prerogatives of authority. Matters were difficult and complicated. As long as Father lived and worked, his income was very high; it exceeded 250,000 crowns a year. And his lifestyle was equally high. There were lots of servants, draft horses, riding horses, and even two or three racing horses; there were parties, home concerts by masters, and luxury travels. Now, all had to be restrained. But this didn't change mother's attitude at all, even when the First World War forced her into exile in a small apartment in Vienna, or when after returning home, the war damages forced her to even more restraint with expenses.

She always enjoyed responsibilities and activity; she loved company around her, commotion and children. And she was always surrounded

---

129 Bertha Pappenheim (1859–1936).

130 Bertha Pappenheim and David Kaufmann, *Die Memoiren der Glückel von Hameln: Geboren in Hamburg 1645, gestorben in Metz 19. September 1724* (Vienna: Verlag von S. Meyer und W. Pappenheim, 1910). Bertha Pappenheim travelled in Galicia, lectured and wrote on the province, especially on the situation of Jewish women. Bertha Pappenheim, *Zur Lage der jüdischen Bevölkerung in Galizien: Reise-Eindrücke und Vorschläge zur Besserung der Verhältnisse* (Frankfurt a. M.: Neuer Frankfurter-Verlag, 1904); idem, *Sisyphus-Arbeit: Reisebriefe aus den Jahren 1911 und 1912* [1. und] 2. Folge (Leipzig [2.F.: Berlin]: Linder [2.F.: Levy], 1929).

131 Karl M. Baer, who used the pseudonym N. O. Body (1885–1956).

132 "Out of a man's maiden years" [M.L.]. N. O. Body, *Aus eines Mannes Mädchenjahren* (Berlin: G. Riecke Nachf., 1907).

33

Emma Lilien née Nierenstein, ca. 1920. Courtesy of Catherine Grun

by people. She either issued orders or she rejoiced looking at the swarm of our cousins and friends. When she returned from some trip, she had much to tell about the antics of little Neapolitan *lazzaroni*,[133] or about the laughing eyes of swarthy Arabian children in Egypt.

Around 1925, the first signs appeared of numbness in her hands. She traveled to the greatest medical authorities in Europe. They diagnosed a gradual dystrophy of muscles and nerves, but couldn't help her. The disease progressed for many years. Towards the end, Mother was almost an invalid and had to be pushed about in a wheelchair.[134]

---

133 The lower class of eighteenth-century Naples.

134 When Mother almost lost the use of her hands, she still used to spend hours on the phone, calling people "in power" to get employment for some poor wretch, or calling people to a meeting for one of the many welfare organizations she headed.

But her mind always remained fresh; her interests were always keen, a ruler, a sovereign, and always ready to help others.

When thinking about mother, I have to paraphrase the well-known verse of Goethe, and it seems to me that

Von Mutter hab' ich die Statur,
Des Lebens ernstes Führen;
Vom Vaeterchen die Frohnatur
Und Lust zum Fabulieren.[135]

THE LILIEN FAMILY

According to the criteria of Jewish patricians, the Liliens were newcomers. For many generations they lived in the little town of Brzozdowce[136] on the river Dniester; some also resided in neighboring Rozdół[137] and Drohobycz.[138] They were petty merchants, artisans, tenants, and traders.

My great-grandfather Moses came to Lwów, unsuccessfully trying to attain some status here. He divorced his wife, tried this and that, and drank. Despite his misfortunes, he allegedly never lost his good humor and kept repeating the old phrase which became a family motto: "Be receptive to joy as a sponge and shed sorrows like a rain cape."

His son, my grandfather Ignacy, was accepted as a boy into the banking business of Jakub Stroh. He worked hard as office help, doing more than his share from dawn to dusk. Very ambitious, his conduct

---

Innumerable meetings were held at our home (with refreshments served). After different experiences with the "Protection of Women," Mother came to the conclusion that you have to start them young; she then concentrated on organizing day-nurseries for the poorest [M.L.].

135 Johann Wolfgang Goethe, *Zahme Xenien* 6: "Vom Vater hab' ich die Statur,/ Des Lebens ernstes Führen,/ Vom Mütterchen die Frohnatur/ Und Lust zu fabulieren" (From my father I have a stature and seriousness of acting, from my dear mother my happy disposition and a delight in telling stories). Lilien's paraphrase means: "From my mother I have a stature and seriousness of acting, from my dear father my happy disposition and a delight in telling stories."

136 Presently Berezdivtsi in Lviv oblast, Ukraine.

137 Presently Rozdil in Lviv oblast, Ukraine.

138 Presently Drohobych in Lviv oblast, Ukraine.

Hetmańska Street in Lwów, "Sokal and Lilien" Bank, 1900.
Courtesy of Lviv Historical Museum

always beyond reproach, he started at the bottom, advanced, and saved money. After many years he became independent and made a career for himself. Together with a co-worker in the office, Sokal, they opened a small banking house and exchange office in Lwów and named it "Sokal and Lilien." He aroused well-deserved confidence in him and gained more and more accounts among the merchants, local gentry, land-owners, clergy, public officers, and institutions. He gave sound advice and conscientiously served his clients. The business developed steadily and in time became the foremost private banking house in the country.

Success never affected Ignacy's lifestyle. He reached the top all on his own, but never behaved like an upstart. He always remained extremely modest and charitable. He nurtured some kind of Evangelic love for mankind and extended a helping hand wherever he could.[139]

---

139 Ignacy Lilien was the president of "Szczera przyjaźń" (Sincere Friendship) society, located in the Skarbek Theater building. See *Ilustrowany skorowidz stołecznego*

Ignacy Lilien. *Courtesy of Catherine Grun*

I frequently met people who spoke with emotion of how grandfather had helped them get on their feet. He never expected gratitude and disliked to be thanked. Often he slipped money into someone's pocket, disappearing quickly, before the recipient could even notice the gesture.

His family life was calm and serene. Granny Blandyna Lilien née Pfeffer was an excellent wife and mother. She was petite, gentle, and smiling, always active and busy, always compassionate. Her serenity and ambition certainly contributed greatly to the success of her husband. One of her uncles, Burstin, an engineer, served in the Austrian navy and attained the rank of admiral. Granny, herself, was modest and

miasta Lwowa z okazyi Powszechnej Wystawy Krajowej roku 1894 (Lwów: Fr. S. Reichman, 1894), 88.

Blandyna Lilien née Pfeffer, second half of nineteenth century.
Courtesy of Catherine Grun

bourgeois; however, very ambitious as far as her husband and sons were concerned.

Their old-fashioned apartment was roomy and warm, but a far cry from being grandiose and pretentious; it was cozy, filled with tenderness. We grandchildren came there frequently. There were always plenty of goodies and sometimes a gift awaited us. Our smiling Granny was always at home. Sometimes some elderly ladies came for a good cup of coffee and some reading aloud.

They had four sons. Uncle Edward was the eldest.[140] Then came my father, Adolf,[141] after him Norbert,[142] the physician, and finally

---

140 Józef Edward Lilien (1862–?).
141 Adolf Lilien (1863–1911).
142 Norbert Jakub Lilien (1869–1940).

Ernest Leon,[143] the economist. They were brought up with care, as Granny believed that a good education was the basis for a successful life. The boys studied diligently, except for the youngest, Lonio, who repeated all along that he was not "made for reading."

Edward and my father were already married when Grandpa purchased seven *morgs*[144] of land in the suburban area of Zofiówka. On this property he built a villa to serve as a summer residence for the whole family.[145] It contained three apartments: one for the grandparents and the two others for their married sons. There were separate rooms for the bachelor sons. Another smaller house left by the previous owners served as the servants' quarters. The surroundings were picturesque, filled with rolling hills and gulches. A brook rustled below and one had to cross over a bridge among old oak trees providing shade for the garden. One of the slopes was covered with a thicket that we called "the grove." There was an orchard on top of the escarpment and beyond were fields and meadows. The ground was cleared, the garden planted, and "Lonio's Avenue of Trees" was started. The house was surrounded by lilacs, jasmines, rosebushes, and blooming cherries. Squirrels, woodpeckers, titmice, and nightingales populated the area. Occasionally one could spot a hare or a ferret. It was paradise.

Every morning, the gentlemen walked to work in the city. They returned home for lunch in horse-driven cabs, which waited to take them back to work in the afternoon. In the meantime, the cabmen were treated to a sandwich and vodka. The gentlemen often brought home some treats for lunch, as well as some guests. A swimming pool with a shower and a cabin was built along the stream and they all went together for a swim before lunch.

Soon, another house was built on the other side of the hill. It was destined for guests and, since there was a stable and a barn nearby, we called it "the farm." There were good riding horses, as well as horses for the carriage.

---

143 Ernest Leon Lilien (1872–?).
144 About ten American acres [M.L.]. One *morg* is 5755 square meters.
145 The actual address of this villa, now changed almost beyond recognition and dilapidated, is 38 Yaroslavenka Street.

39

Lilien's villa in Zofiówka, 1903. *Courtesy of Catherine Grun*

Such was the life of Grandfather Ignacy. He lived in this happy era when wars and upheavals were forgotten, when it was understood that man was protected by law and lived free of fear or want. Grandfather did not look for honor; he helped others and loved his family life. In my memory, his life remained like an idyllic painting of *A Good Man's Life*.[146]

Grandfather Ignacy was a Freemason. A compass and a trowel were engraved on his gravestone. I inherited from him a paperweight with the same emblem. He must have been especially appreciated in the Masonic circle. When I was once introduced to Mr. Heltai Ferenc,[147] the mayor of the city of Budapest, he asked me whether I was the son of Ignacy Lilien.

"I am his grandson."

"You are a grandson of my brother."

---

146 Title of a sixteenth-century treatise in Polish literature [M.L.] Mikołaj Rej (1505–1569) wrote his *Żywot człowieka poczciwego* (1567) as the first part of *Źwierciadło, albo Kształt, w którym każdy stan snadnie się może swym sprawam jako we źwierciedle przypatrzyć* (Kraków, 1567–1568).

147 Heltai Ferenc (1861–1913), a writer, politician, and mayor of Budapest.

He hugged me, invited me to his house and paid me a lot of attention. I received a similar reception from Mr. von Anhauch,[148] a rich Jew in Czernowitz.

The portrait of my grandfather, with his blond sideburns and a pair of good, wise, blue eyes, was hanging in the most important place—on the wall of my living room at Zofiówka. He was the founder of our [house at] Zofiówka.

There is an interesting legend connected with the origins of the Liliens, those humble Jews from Brzozdowce. One gravestone in the old Jewish cemetery in that inland provincial town bears the inscription with the name of Mechel Lilien. It dates from the times of Sigismund III Vasa, and Mechel was executed by some tribunal of inquisition. During my lifetime, the local Jewish population regarded the monument with respect and every year assembled there for prayers.

A romantic story was passed on to me from diverse sources about Mechel Lilien. Allegedly, he was a German knight, Michael von Lilien. He fell in love with a German Jewess from Swabia and wanted to marry her. She consented under the condition that he convert to Judaism. There was, however, a death penalty for defection from the Christian faith. He therefore left his country, abandoned his title, position, and wealth and emigrated with her to Poland, known for religious tolerance. He had no way of knowing that precisely at that time, under the Jesuit influence of the regime of King Sigismund, the situation of the Jews in Poland would deteriorate.

After the wedding, he leased Brzozdowce from Count Rzewuski and began a new life. Lady Rzewuska was stimulated by the presence of this romantic foreigner and tried to attract him by doing many favors. Michael, however, loved his wife, for whom he had sacrificed so much. He remained faithful to her and insensible to the advances of the strange lady. In her disappointment, the other woman brought the Jesuits upon him. He was accused of abandoning his faith, condemned, and decapitated.

When departing for his last voyage, he is said to have consoled his lamenting family with the following words:

---

148 Max von Anhauch (1863–1945), knighted in 1917, an industrialist.

"Don't cry and always remember to be receptive to joy as a sponge and shed sorrows like a rain cape."

Some Lilien barons from Belgium studied the family genealogy and exchanged letters on this subject with my uncle Edward. Although I never found out whether my ancestor Mechel was the same person as Michael, the knight, I became interested in the genealogy of those Lilien barons. The oldest known document was a contract signed by Theodorich von der Lilie in Woerl, in the year 1328. They were "robber knights" in the Rhineland. First, they signed their name Von der Lilie, later Reichsritter von Lilien, and finally they received the title of Baron and signed their name as "Freiherr von Lilien."

I heard an old legend, laced with a romantic love affair, by which in the remote Middle Ages they moved to Germany from France, where they used to be called du Lys or Mont du Lys. Probably as a result of this migration came the motto: *"Quo Deus esse iussit."*[149]

Hence, it seems that a thousand years ago, from French they became Germans, then Polish Jews some three hundred years ago, and who knows if nowadays these Polish Jews will not become British or Americans.

Quo Deus esse iussit.

However, this time it is not romantic love that will bring about the change. But whatever happens, we must not forget our ancient heritage. From the old Liliens we inherited our blue eyes, we have their blond hair, their features, their happy, sunny disposition, and we also have their guiding words:

"Be receptive to joy as a sponge and shed sorrows like a rain cape."

MY FATHER

ADOLF LILIEN, son of Ignacy, born in 1863, died in 1911

He was a good child growing up in a loving home, strong and sturdy, with a head of blond hair and a frank, open look. His Jewish friends

---

149 What God commands you to be.

Adolf Lilien, 1888. *Courtesy of Catherine Grun*

called him "a peasant" because he did not look Jewish to them. He was straightforward, without hidden thoughts. He despised ruse and craftiness. If someone offended him, he would hit back. However, he was loved and no one would want to offend him. A good student, he loved to read, was involved in sports, and [took] long hikes.

After graduating from high school he did a year of military service in the 24th Austrian Infantry Battalion at Kołomyja.[150] He soon became an officer in the reserves and always praised his period of military service. He never experienced war.

---

150 A small town in southeast Poland [M.L.]. Presently Kolomyia in Ivano-Frankivsk oblast, Ukraine. Kołomyja was a secondary seat of the "k.u.k. Galizisch-Bukowinisches Infanterie Regiment 'Ritter von Kummer' Nr. 24," initially founded in 1629.

43

He studied Law at the University of Lwów, where he received his doctoral degree. He was liked by his fellow students.

It was a liberal era, when religious differences did not affect human relations in any way. A movement of assimilation began spreading among the Jewish population. Smolka[151] devised and enforced the slogan of equal rights. The Jews accepted the friendly hand that the Gentiles extended them. This movement was meant to propagate the Polish spirit among the Jewish population, to integrate into the Polish nation those who for ages had lived in separate ghettos, and to draw together the Jews with the rest of society.

My father became one of the pioneers of this movement. He vividly participated in all activities of Polish students. He was a co-founder and vice-president of the Czytelnia Akademicka (Academic Reading Club) which, unfortunately, in my time became a nest of antisemitism. In his time, however, it was a center of progress and free thinking. He was also a member and co-founder of a sports club named Sokół (Falcon), which was the first paramilitary organization in Poland. The "Falcons" wore sand-colored uniforms decorated with cords and modeled on a *czamara*,[152] purplish-red shirts, and caps adorned by a large falcon feather. Such a uniform was given to me when I was four years old. When I wore it, the street urchins teased me: "Look, look, here comes a sparrow, not a falcon!"

At the same time, my father was also one of the founders of the Przymierze Braci (Fraternal Alliance),[153] an organization of Polish and Jewish students. The objective of the Alliance was to propagate the Polish spirit among the Jewish masses. They published a magazine

---

151 Franciszek Jan Smolka (1810–1899), a Polish lawyer, liberal politician, president of the Reichstag in Kremsier in the revolutionary years 1848–1849, and president of the Austrian Imperial Council in 1881–1893.
152 *Czamara* is a Polish upper dress of Hungarian origin.
153 "Agudas Achim" (Heb. Agudat Aḥim), "Przymierze Braci." Adolf Lilien was influential in Agudat Aḥim, the most prominent center of assimilation, where he was opposed to the transition of the *Hamazkir* newspaper from Hebrew to Polish. See Rachel Manekin, "The Debate over Assimilation in Late Nineteenth-Century Lwów," in *Insiders and Outsiders*, ed. Richard I. Cohen, Jonathan Frankel, and Stefani Hoffman (Oxford: Littman Library of Jewish Civilization, 2010), 124.

entitled *Ojczyzna* (Fatherland), traveled, lectured, and organized classes, while the members of the Alliance taught the Polish language to Jewish children. Father was personally involved in this effort. He lectured, and one of his students was Wilhelm Feldman,[154] who came to Lwów as a poor Orthodox boy, wearing a Jewish caftan, very eager to learn and to acquire knowledge of Polish. He later became a famous writer known for his literary essays.

The organization was later joined by some renowned men, such as Romanowicz,[155] Rutowski,[156] the mayor of the city of Lwów during the war of 1914–1918, and Stesłowicz,[157] who became the minister of the Postal Services and president of the Chamber of Commerce of Lwów.

Alfred Nossig,[158] an eccentric distant cousin of my father, also joined the organization. He was so ostentatiously patriotic that he always wore black as a sign of mourning after the downfall of the 1863 insurrection. He wrote a novel entitled *John the Prophet*,[159] in which he is the prophet and my father is "Franek, extending a white, warm muscular hand." Nossig underwent a sudden metamorphosis. He unexpectedly became a fervent Zionist and emigrated from Poland. He was a writer and a sculptor. He befriended Paderewski,[160] carved a good profile sculpture of this great master, and wrote the libretto for his opera *Manru*.[161] In his old age, he was overcome by mysticism and intended to redeem mankind with his writings. He emerged in Poland again, an old man, deprived of all means of livelihood when escaping from Hitler. In memory of my father, I gave him shelter, inviting him to live at Zofiówka. He was constantly writing something, stating that one must have self-discipline in order to create a masterpiece.

---

154 Wilhelm Feldman (1868–1919), a journalist, literary critic, and historian.
155 Tadeusz Romanowicz (1843–1904), a member of the Polish national movement in Galicia, political prisoner, and writer.
156 Tadeusz Klemens Rutowski (1852–1918), a politician, journalist, and patron of culture.
157 Władysław Stesłowicz (1867–1940), a lawyer, politician, minister of posts and telegraph, and Diet member.
158 Alfred Nossig (1864–1943), a sculptor, musician, writer, and public activist.
159 Alfred Nossig, *Jan Prorok: Opowieść na tle galicyjskim z 1880 r. w dziewięciu księgach* (Lwów: Księgarnia polska, 1892).
160 Ignacy Jan Paderewski (1860–1941), a Polish pianist, composer, and politician.
161 *Manru* was written ca. 1901.

Hetmańska Street in Lwów, 1920s. The Office of Internal Revenue and the Jesuit Church on the left, the Viennese Café in the center, and the new building of the Union Bank (formerly Sokal and Lilien) on the right.
Courtesy of Igor Kotlobualtov Collection

He wanted to convince me to join him in his mystical endeavors. He used to say: "I am a prophet. Humanity produces occasionally a Messiah and I am one of them right now. A prophet needs apostles and you should become my apostle."

My father adhered faithfully to the path he had chosen in his youth. During his student years, and later in his professional life, he was primarily trying to be a good citizen. He always said that a man must make himself useful.

After my grandfather died, my father took over his bank, Sokal & Lilien. He inspired confidence in people—a trait he inherited from grandfather—and he developed the bank most successfully. He financed and arranged loans on behalf of the city of Lwów and offered his initiative and credits toward the industrialization of Galicia. He built the Lwów-Brzeżany-Podhajce railroad,[162] maintained control over the petroleum business, as well as lumber, building, and real estate. He even tackled some international trade by organizing the export of eggs from Riga to Manchester. Toward the end of his life, father's personal yearly income exceeded 250,000 crowns.

---

162 Presently Lviv-Berezhany-Pidhaitsi. Presently only a short segment of this line is active.

Chamber of Commerce on Akademicka Street. Postcard, 1918.
Courtesy of Museum of Ancient Ukrainian Book Art, the Borys Voznytsky
National Art Gallery of Lviv

Despite many opportunities and invitations, he never aspired to enter politics; however, he always supported and voted for the candidates of his choice. He, himself, was only vice-president of the local Chamber of Commerce and one of the original initiators of the construction of its beautiful building in the heart of the city on Akademicka Street.[163] He was an auditor of the Savings Bank of Galicia, and together with Prince Andrzej Lubomirski,[164] they founded the Central Union of Industrialists. He never accepted Austrian medals of honor that were offered him; he told me that the only honor he would be happy to accept would be the honorary citizenship of the City of Lwów. This honor, however, was never bestowed upon him.[165]

All business was meaningless to him unless it was transacted with some community welfare in mind. In 1906, Russia issued a large-scale international loan and it was proposed that my father act as their agent for Galicia. He refused on principle.[166]

---

163 Presently Shevchenka Avenue.
164 Andrzej Lubomirski (1862–1953), a member of parliament, literary agent, industrialist, and politician.
165 Among the few things that were saved from Hitler during World War II is a beautiful leather-bound and silver-decorated document, written and illuminated on parchment. It was presented to my grandfather, Adolf Lilien, with thanks and recognition by the Jewish community. This document has been donated to and is displayed at the Jewish Museum of New York [J.G.].
166 Since Russia was Poland's enemy [M.L.].

Adolf Lilien, 1909, Lwów. According to family reminiscences, the dog did not belong to Adolf Lilien, it just loved to be photographed.
Courtesy of Catherine Grun

He dedicated a large portion of his income to welfare and humanitarian causes. I don't know the details because he never talked much about it. I only know that he founded a summer camp for needy Jewish schoolchildren in Dębina[167] near Skole in the Carpathian Mountains. I also know that he always contributed on a large scale to good causes. Many people told me that they owed their entire career to my father.

Two of his brothers were great financial burdens on him. Edward, who lived much above his means, cost father quite a lot. Ernest Leon,

---

167 Presently Dubyna in Lviv oblast, Ukraine.

modest and hard working, liked to fantasize and was unsuccessful in business, while my father paid his debts. After my father died and they had nobody to lean on, both my uncles emigrated to America.

Father worked too hard. He carried on without a stop from early morning till late at night. He took only a short break for lunch. Even on Sundays and holidays he spent the mornings in his office. However, he said that during his free time "he locked all thoughts of business in a drawer" and devoted himself wholeheartedly to family life, friends, and fun.

At such times he was happy and gay. Early in the morning he would go horse riding. When I grew a bit, he took me along. Guests came to our house almost every evening. He loved music and often organized concerts when occasionally great masters such as Paderewski, Rosenthal,[168] or d'Albert[169] played in our home. Teodor Pollak,[170] the genius disciple of Liszt,[171] was a friend of my father and showed up regularly. Father liked to dance too. He gave balls in our house and himself was a ringleader in the Mazurka, Cotillion, and Quadrille. I remember that once, after the fifth figure of a Quadrille, he led all the guests, couple by couple into the hall, ordered them to put on their fur coats, and then downstairs into the street where a long line of horse-driven sleighs were waiting to take them all to Brzuchowice,[172] a small resort town eight kilometers away. There, another warm bright ballroom was ready and dancing continued till morning.

Every year father allowed himself to take a one-month vacation. When I was small, he went to the mountains by himself—mostly to the Austrian Alps—where he wandered alone with a knapsack on his back, never stopping for longer than a day or two. On his way, he sang and

---

168 Moriz Rosenthal (1862–1946), a skilled Polish pianist.
169 Eugène Francis Charles d'Albert (1864–1932), a Scottish-born German pianist and composer.
170 Teodor Pollak (1866–1916), a composer and pianist, professor at the Ludwik Marek School of Music in Lwów; in later years Pollak founded there his own school of music.
171 Franz Liszt (1811–1886), a Hungarian composer, virtuoso pianist, conductor, and teacher.
172 Presently Bryukhovychi in Lviv oblast, Ukraine.

composed happy poems which he mailed to mother. When I was ten years old, he took me along on his hike. Three years later, when my sister Klara was ten, he took both of us together. This time we went to the Tatra Mountains and spent a wonderful month of mountain excursions. Later, father usually traveled with mother and less frequently went on his hiking expeditions.

While leading such an intensive life, he still found time to do some amateur writing. He admired the opera *The Haunted Manor* by Moniuszko.[173] He translated its entire libretto in verse into German and tried to have this opera produced in Vienna and Munich.

He enjoyed good paintings and sculpture and every year added some works of art to his private collection. Among his most valuable ones was a large canvas by Kaczor-Batowski[174] representing the attack of the Winged Polish Hussars at Chocim.[175] There existed many reproductions of this famous painting and it was even printed on postcards. Father also often bought paintings by lesser artists, saying that one must support the beginning talents.

The eccentric lawyer Leon Jekeles belonged to the circle of father's friends.[176] He was tall and bony, with a thick beard. He spoke in a deep voice and had the manner of a provincial nobleman. He was a descendant of one of the few Jewish families who were closely linked with old Polish history. In the district of Kraków called Kazimierz, there is the Jekeles Synagogue dating from the fifteenth century.[177] One Father Długosz,[178] a priest, historian, and tutor to the royal Jagiellonian

---

173 Stanisław Moniuszko (1819–1872), a Polish composer, conductor, and teacher. He composed his opera *Straszny dwór* (The Haunted Manor) in ca. 1861–1864.
174 Stanisław Kaczor-Batowski (1866–1946), a Polish painter.
175 Chocim is presently Khotyn in Chernivtsi oblast, Ukraine.
176 I remember him well. When I was a little girl, he always came to Seder at my grandmother's house. On other occasions he spent many hours sitting and talking to grandmother, who was in a wheelchair [J.G.].
177 The Ajzyk Synagogue, at 16 Kupa Street in Krakow, was built in 1638 as a private foundation by one of the most affluent Kraków Jews at the time, *kahal* elder Isaac Jakubowicz (reb Ajzyk reb Jekeles).
178 Jan Długosz (1415–1480, also known as Joannes Longinus or Dlugossius), a Polish priest, chronicler, diplomat, soldier, and secretary to Bishop Zbigniew Oleśnicki of Kraków.

princes,[179] was involved in a lawsuit with one of the Jekeles for a lot of land on which today stands the famous ancient Jagiellonian University. During the 1863 Polish insurrection against Russia, Leon's elder brother, Maurycy Jekeles, served as a commissary of the Polish National Government for the district of Tarnopol.[180]

Once, a rural squire wanted to pay a compliment to Leon Jekeles and remarked that he spoke perfect Polish; to this, indignant Leon retorted: "It is not strange at all that my Polish is good. I studied at universities and I speak in the courts of law. I do have a piece of land, but I dwell in the city among cultured people. It is strange, however, that you speak Polish so well, since you live in the country and I suppose something is missing in your education."

When at the next table in a cafe someone criticized Jews aloud, Leon, in his deep, loud voice declared: "But you made a Jewess the queen of the Polish Crown and you pray to her in Częstochowa."[181]

Another interesting friend of father's was Mr. Jodko-Narkiewicz,[182] the president of the revolutionary faction of the Polish Socialist Party. He was an elegant country squire from Lithuania, owner of a famous library, and a fervent political activist. He always stayed at our house when he came to Lwów on "conspirators' business."

My father's life, however, was not at all carefree. He was deeply concerned about his brothers. He was also very worried, maybe too much so, about my own independent and often rebellious temperament. He took it too much to heart when, as a very young man, I decided to marry without the consent of my family. After two years of delaying, when I was twenty-one years old, my father reluctantly, with heavy heart, finally agreed. I went to Vienna, where I was to meet my English fiancée and together, via Algiers and Morocco, we were to proceed to her father in Liverpool, where the wedding was to take

---

179 Jagiellons: the Polish royal family [J.G.]. The Jagiellonian dynasty reigned in 1386–1572.
180 Presently Ternopil in Ukraine.
181 Alluding to the Black St. Mary of Częstochowa—the object of Polish pilgrimage [J.G.].
182 Witold Jodko-Narkiewicz (1864–1924), who wrote under the pseudonyms A. Wroński and Jowisz, a Polish socialist, journalist, and diplomat.

place. However, in Vienna some differences arose and we broke up the engagement. But father never knew about it. Almost at the same time I received a telegram from Lwów announcing his sudden death. It was a terrible blow. He was so beautiful, so happy, and so full of joy. He was only forty-seven years old. Overwork combined with worries about his brothers—and maybe I, too, added to his bitterness. I immediately cut short my trip and returned to Lwów, still in time for the funeral. I could never stop blaming myself for not being good enough to my beloved father. He always gave in to happiness, and when he was happy, it was wholeheartedly. He resisted all worries and never showed them. But the tension was too strong and the dear heart gave in. The doctors tried to appease my remorse and reassured me that his illness had been progressing for some years. However, I never forgave myself and never experienced peace of mind.

After Father's death, serious troubles developed in the family. The balance of his accounts amounted to about 20 million crowns. There were properties in Hnilice,[183] Rożdżałów,[184] and Dziewięcierz,[185] altogether about 5,000 *morgs* of land with forests, lumber yards, and distilleries. There was the bank, a five-story building at 12 Hetmańska Street, and several building lots. There was the glass factory at Żółkiew and shares in the petroleum business. On the other hand, he left large monetary obligations toward the Viennese Union Bank as well as private investors. I was only twenty-one years old; therefore, mother referred all business matters to the attorney Klemens Sokal, who started selling out on a big scale. Union Bank took over our family bank and made it its branch in Lwów. After the restoration of Poland, it became Bank Unji w Polsce, S.A. we Lwowie (The Union Bank in Poland, Ltd. in Lwów). In accordance with the contract, the huge sum of money received for the bank was deposited for ten years in our account at the new branch, while we drew only the interest. Meanwhile came the First World War with the monetary crash and a rapid devaluation of currency. Consequently, in 1921, when the huge amount

---

183 Presently Hnylytsi in Ternopil oblast, Ukraine.
184 Presently Rozzhaliv in Lviv oblast, Ukraine.
185 Presently Devyatyr in Lviv oblast, Ukraine

of money was released, all I could buy with it was a pack of cigarettes. Similar was the fate of our land and other properties, which were sold for Austrian crowns on long-term payments and were completely consumed by the devaluation.

There remained only the house at Hetmańska, the glass factory, and Zofiówka. Mother had the house at Sykstuska left to her by her father. These were still of some value. Then came difficult times and hardships. The Polish economy was in bad shape. The country was threatened from both sides by enemy neighbors. Taxes were high, government welfare institutions too spendthrift, and thus the remainder of our estate continued to melt away.

MY UNCLES AND THEIR CHILDREN

Dr. Edward Lilien was a flashy personality, highly educated, with charming manners. He was an outstanding attorney and member of the City Council of Lwów. A mismatched wife, however, was poisoning his life. He avoided coming home and started to spend more money than he could afford. When my father died and there was nobody who would pay his debts, he left for America. There, of necessity, he worked very hard and finally stood on his own two feet while managing an attorney's office in New York. He also translated into English *Eros and Psyche*, a drama by the Polish writer Żuławski.[186]

His daughter Wanda was very beautiful and very well educated. She studied history and earned a PhD degree in this field. She married Professor Olgierd Górka[187] whom she later divorced. She worked for the Port Authority of Gdańsk, where she attained a high executive

---

186 Jerzy Żuławski (1874–1915), *Eros i Psyche: Powieść sceniczna w siedmiu rozdziałach* (Lwów: H. Altenberg, 1904); it was impossible to locate the English translation in available bibliographical sources and apparently never published. Edward Lilien also published a book, *Easy Method for Learning Polish Quickly: A New System on the Most Simple Principles for Universal Self-Tuition, with Complete English Pronunciation of Every Word* (New York: Wehman Bros., 1914).

187 Olgierd Aleksander Górka (1887–1955), a Polish historian, journalist, politician, and diplomat.

53

position. But above all, she devoted her time and energy toward a perfect upbringing of her daughter Danusia,[188] a beautiful girl in every respect. Danusia married Bertie Tauszyński,[189] an engineer, and remained in Warsaw with her mother and child[190] when World War II broke out.

Edward's second daughter, Jadwiga, married a Polish-American named Rynas. She now lives in the USA and has two sons who are serving in the American army.

Edward's son, Tadeusz, was a good-looking and intelligent young man. He served in the Polish Legion during the First World War. He married and had children, but lived a disorderly life and died young.

Dr. Norbert Lilien, a physician, was an honest, quiet, respectable man, and a gentleman without blemish.[191] He was very close to us and when he became a widower, he married my widowed mother in the late years of her life. He died recently in Lwów under the Russian occupation.

His daughter Olga took after grandmother Blandyna.[192] She was quiet, always busy, and would always try to be helpful to others. In fact,

---

188   Anna Danuta Tauszyńska (ca. 1916–1994), a translator from German to Polish. Danusia died in Warsaw in June 1994. I visited her in Poland in 1987, after fifty years of absence. She and her husband Bertie, a charming elderly couple, gave me a wonderful reception. My daughter Catherine, to whom this book is dedicated, also went to Poland, met Danusia and Bertie, and became friends with their son Christopher [J.G.].

189   Robert Tauszyński (1910–1997).

190   Krzysztof Piotr Tauszyski (1938–2012), an architect.

191   Norbert Jakub Lilien (1869–1940) was a pediatrician; he also engaged in artistic photography. See Aleksander Żakowicz, *Fotografia galicyjska do roku 1918: Fotografowie Galicji, Tatr oraz Księstwa Cieszyńskiego* (Lwów: "Centrum Europy," 2008), 80.

192   Olga Blanka Lilien (1903, Lwów–1996, Tarnobrzeg), daughter of Norbert Lilien and Joanna née Braun. Finishing her medical studies, she interned for one year in the United States at a hospital in Terre Haute, Indiana. She practiced pediatric medicine for the next year and a half in Berlin, followed by a year in Paris, finally returning to Lwów. Olga then began teaching hygiene at the same high school she had attended as a girl. By the outbreak of World War II, she was also assisting in the bacteriological research laboratory of Dr. Henryk Meisel (1894–1981). She was rescued by a righteous Polish woman, Barbara Makuch, during the Holocaust. See Humboldt.edu, accessed 13 December 2014, http://www.humboldt.edu/rescuers/book/Makuch/olga/Olga.html.

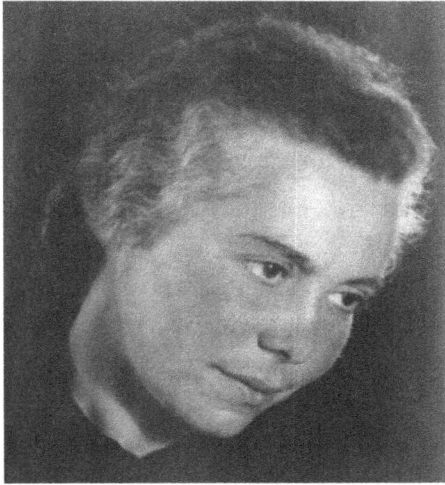

Doctor Olga Lilien, 1938. *Courtesy of POLIN Museum of the History of Polish Jews, "Polish Righteous—Recalling Forgotten History"*

she contributed most in the upbringing of my own daughter, for which I am most grateful to her. She was also a physician. Lately,[193] she was managing a laboratory in Lwów in which vaccines were produced.

This particular specialization saved her life under the Russian and German occupation. Her vaccines were urgently needed, therefore they left her alone. I wonder what is happening to her now. A new wave of destruction has hit our beloved Lwów. I have the feeling, however, that of all our relatives, she had the best chance of survival.[194]

Norbert's younger daughter, Helenka, also remained in Lwów.[195]

Ernest Leon Lilien was a charming, original, person. He managed Dom dla Ziemian (House of Landowners) in Lwów, but went bankrupt and left for Canada. At the onset of the 1914 war, he was interned as an Austrian citizen. While living in a deserted spot together with some other Polish and Ukrainian peasants from Galicia, he founded a

---

193 Just before the war [J.G.].
194 Olga lives in Tarnobrzeg, Poland. I visited her in December 1987. She is now about ninety years old, grew smaller with age, always a dear, helping everyone around. Our meeting was very sentimental [J.G.].
195 She did not survive the war. Nobody has heard of her [J.G.].

settlement and called it "Lilienvillage."[196] Later, he moved to the USA and became a journalist. I think that he played at being a radical. He refused a well paid agency for the Canadian Pacific Railway. He hoped to make his fortune on some new method to eradicate rats, which was a fiasco, of course. When Poland officially acknowledged the occupation of Manchuria, he wrote a letter of protest to President Mościcki.[197] I saw him for the last time when he came to Poland to attend a convention of Poles from abroad as a representative of the American Polonia. For many years, he has been working on a huge Polish-English dictionary of which he sent me the first volume comprising a small part of the letter "A."[198] I like him and would welcome a chance to see him again.

His wife, Emma née Czeszer, was a singer and to this day has preserved her youthful energy and temperament. She is pleasant, full of interests; she managed to escape from the Bolsheviks and is now in America.[199]

Ernest's daughter, Zofia, who married Stande,[200] is a second copy of Grandmother Blandyna in my generation. She finished the Horticultural College in Holland and Switzerland. She fell in love and married a communist poet. Her husband spent years in various European prisons,[201] and she followed him and lived in whatever place he was kept. For years she kept bringing food to him in jail and when he was finally freed he left her and their small child, Olga, and moved to Moscow.

---

196 Lilienville, near the Centre d'interprétation Camp, Spirit Lake, Quebec, Canada.
197 Ignacy Mościcki (1867–1946), a Polish chemist, politician, and president of Poland (1926–1939).
198 Ernest Lilien, *Dictionary*, vol. 1 (Buffalo: Dziennik dla wszystkich, 1944).
199 She passed away in the 1960s [J.G.].
200 Stanisław Ryszard Stande (1897, Warsaw–1 November 1937, Moscow), a Polish poet, activist of the Communist Party of Poland, of which he was a member since 1923. He studied philosophy at the Jagiellonian University. He was one of editors of *Miesięcznik Literacki* in 1929–1931. In 1931 he moved to the USSR, where he edited the *Internatsional'naia Literatura* magazine. He was executed in Moscow under the Stalinist repressions and was rehabilitated in 1955. Stande published books: *Rzeczy i ludzie* (Kraków: Drukarnia Narodowa, 1925); *Molodezh' idet* (Moscow: OGIZ, 1933); *Stikhi* (Moscow: Litizdat, 1935). His second wife was Soviet pianist Maria Grinberg (1908–1978).
201 This might be greatly exaggerated by Artur. In fact, he left for the USSR where he was recognized as a good writer [J.G.].

Zofia returned to Poland and worked as an instructor in the experimental agricultural center in Fredrów.[202] Later, she lost her hearing and came to live in my house in Żółkiew, devoting her time meticulously looking after my home and garden, raising her daughter, and poring over her microscope, selecting seeds, etc. The last news I had of her and her daughter was that they were "working on the land." I loved her like a sister. Hopefully God will save her.[203]

Zofia had two brothers. The elder, Ignacy,[204] held a good position as a chemical engineer in Holland. He married and had several children. At the same time, he distinguished himself as a prominent musician and composer. He wrote a few operas, which were performed in London and Paris. One of them was composed to the text by George Bernard Shaw,[205] with whom he was on friendly terms. I wonder what has become of him.

Zofia's younger brother, Kazimierz Kajetan,[206] left for America with his father when he was young and that's where he was raised. He has children and is quite well off. He recently organized a family reunion of all members who live in the United States. They all wrote to me and I was surprised to see so many signatures of people close to me. The letterhead showed a pretty picture of his "Chimney House."

Ephraim Moses Lilien, a well-known Jewish painter, was our distant relative. As a young boy, he approached my grandfather Ignacy and asked for support in realizing his dream to become a painter. Grandfather sent him to the Academy of Fine Arts in Kraków and later to Munich. He settled in Berlin, but we always kept in close contact. I even had a few of his drawings dedicated to me. He married a person

---

202 Near Warsaw [J.G.].
203 Toward the end of the war, her nerves gave way and she committed suicide. Her daughter Olga lives in Łódź, Poland. She teaches mathematics in high school and writes mathematics textbooks. She visited us in America and I saw her during my trip to Poland [J.G.].
204 Ignace (Ignacy) Lilien (1897–1964).
205 "The Great Catherine," premiered in Wiesbaden (1932). Irish dramatist George Bernard Shaw (1856–1950) wrote his one-act play *Great Catherine: Whom Glory Still Adores* in 1913.
206 Kazimierz Kajetan Lilien (1903–?).

Offspring of Ignacy Lilien. Genealogical tree, drawing by Marya Lilien-Czarnecka. *Courtesy of Catherine Grun*

from a distinguished old family ("Hoffjuden" at the court of the princes of Brunswick)[207] and they had two children, Otto and Hannah. He was famous for his black-and-white drawings and etchings and especially for his Bible illustrations and those for "The Songs of the Ghetto."[208]

ARTUR LILIEN-BRZOZDOWIECKI, born 1890

I was the first child of young parents in love. They were happy when I was born. Old Majer Rachmiel Mises looked at his fair, blue eyed

---

207 Ephraim Moses Lilien (1874, Drohobycz–1925, Badenweiler) married Helene Emma Magnus (1880–1971) at Braunschweig in 1906. Information supplied by Tom Peters.
208 Morris Rosenfeld, *Lieder des Ghetto*, translated from the Yiddish by Berthold Feiwel with drawings by E. M. Lilien (Berlin: B. Harz, 1902).

Artur, Marya, and Klara Lilien, 1903, Zofiówka.
Courtesy of Catherine Grun

great-great-grandchild and recalled an old Jewish saying that whoever lives to see his fifth generation is assured of a place in Paradise.

I grew up happily. The family spent winters in the city and summers at Zofiówka. At Sykstuska, one room was set aside for me as my gym, furnished with a ladder, a swing, and rings. My earliest memory is watching wood choppers working in the backyard. I was three years old when my sister Klara was born. I then stated very seriously that I was glad to have a sister because I would have a helper in cutting wood and carrying it to the cellar. The summers at Zofiówka were wonderful. The number of cousins was growing and together we were running in the fields, playing war, besieging the fortress; at times we played Indians, at other times cops and robbers. We made escapades to the railroad tracks at Persenkówka,[209] to the guard house, to the race track, or even further up to the forest of Zubrza. When we were a little older, a tennis court was built for us! And not far away there was a large swimming pool in the midst of wooded hills—our beloved Żelazna Woda.[210]

I was wild and unruly. My parents were influenced by the theories of Ellen Key in *Century of the Child*[211] and were happy to let me do anything I wanted. I was healthy and strong. I was beating up the boys in the park and with all this I was not stupid at all. When I was eight years old, a carpentry shop was set up for me at home, where Mr. Szafrański,[212] a master cabinet maker, came every day to teach me for an hour. Under his guidance, I constructed a few objects which were kept in the house as souvenirs.

I attended an unusual elementary school. There were in Lwów two Lithuanian sisters, Mrs. Czarnowska[213] and Mrs. Dalecka,[214] whose father fought in the 1863 insurrection. Their property was confiscated by the Russians. They established a school in the middle of a great park, in the vicinity of the citadel. There were only a few children attending each class. The teachers were excellent and the children came from good homes, mostly landed proprietors or professors. I remember the Pawlewskis,[215] Szczepanowskis,[216] Dybowskis,[217] Ramułts,[218] Klemensiewiczs,[219] and Nusbaums.[220]

---

209 Presently Persenkivka.

210 That's where later I learned to swim and spent many happy hours with my friend [J.G.]. Zalizna Voda: see above, note 114.

211 Ellen Key (1849–1926), *Century of the Child* (London: G. P. Putnam's Sons, 1909).

212 Ludwik Szafrański, a carpenter, lived at 23 Sykstuska Street in 1913; see *Księga adresowa Król. Stoł. Miasta Lwowa. Rocznik 17. 1913; Adress- u. Geschäfts-Handbuch von Lemberg. 17. Jg. 1913* (Lwów: Fr. Reichman, 1913), 415.

213 Józefa Czarnowska, the owner of an educational institution in 1913; see ibid., 71.

214 Wanda Dalecka, an author and teacher; see Antoni Chołoniewski, *Niesmiertelni: Fotografie literatów* (Lwów: n.p., 1898), 98.

215 Bronisław Pawlewski (1886–1915), rector of the Lwów Polytechnic School; see above, note 121.

216 Stanisław Szczepanowski (1846–1900), a member of the Austrian parliament and the Sejm of Galicia, engineer, economy analyst, and oil industrialist.

217 Benedykt Dybowski (1833–1930), a Polish naturalist, traveler, and explorer.

218 Stefan Ramułt (1859–1913), a Polish linguist.

219 Zygmunt Aleksander Klemensiewicz (1886–1963), a Polish physicist and professor at the Lwów Polytechnic School.

220 Józef Nusbaum-Hilarowicz (1859–1917), a Polish zoologist, founder of the Lwów School of Zoology.

Polish eagles were displayed on the walls as well as portraits of Polish kings, Kościuszko,[221] Poniatowski,[222] the Battle of Vienna,[223] the Prussian Homage,[224] the Battle of Racławice[225]—and among these there was an old gun and a pair of commemorative pistols. It all gave off an air of romantic patriotism.

It was obvious to me that it was my milieu and that was where I belonged. Here I began to form my attitude toward society and public affairs.

We had a French governess called Mademoiselle Marguerite. I completed my fourth grade at the Evangelic school where we were taught in German. Thus, as a child, I already spoke fluently in French and German. Later there was an English governess at home. I learned Italian and Russian as an adult.

When I was ten, I went to the Brothers' Bernardine high school, where, like in my elementary school, a strong patriotic spirit prevailed. In Galicia under the Austrian regime, the school system had complete autonomy and was purely Polish. A saying persisted that Polish schools were twisting the minds of young people, preparing them to be servants of Austria. But this was far from the truth. Both the curriculum and the spirit of the teachers, as well as the entire atmosphere, were those of an independent nation. The teachers placed great emphasis on creating a patriotic feeling and all the Polish national holidays were observed.

---

221 Tadeusz Kościuszko (1746–1818), a Polish military engineer, military leader, and national hero.

222 Stanisław II August Poniatowski (1732–1798), the last king and Grand Duke of the Polish-Lithuanian Commonwealth (1764–1795).

223 In the Battle of Vienna (1683), the league of the Holy Roman Empire of the German Nation and the Polish-Lithuanian Commonwealth defeated the Ottoman Empire. King Jan III Sobieski, sending the message of victory to the Pope, was represented in painting by Jan Matejko in 1882–1883 (today this canvas is a highlight of the Vatican Museums).

224 Prussian Homage (1525) was the formal investment of Albert of Prussia as duke of the Polish fief of Ducal Prussia. A canvas on this subject was painted by Jan Matejko in 1882 (today in the Sukiennice Museum, Kraków).

225 Battle of Racławice (1794) was a battle of the Polish Kościuszko uprising against Russia. A cycloramic canvas on this subject was painted by Jan Styka and Wojciech Kossak in 1893–1894 and exhibited in a special pavilion at the Universal Exhibition of 1894 in Lwów (today in the National Museum in Wrocław).

As far as education was concerned, it was on a much higher level than it was later, in the years 1919–1939, when Poland was independent.

In the part of Poland that was under Russian occupation, the schools were Russian and any Polish patriotic thought was stifled. There, the youth had to form secret societies in order to clandestinely learn Polish history and literature and to uphold the Polish spirit, as well as maintain the revolutionary flame. Similar organizations were formed also in Galicia, where they spread propaganda for independence and social reforms. The teachers were well aware of these organizations for "self-education" but deliberately tolerated them.

One of my colleagues at that time was Ferdek Goetel, later a well-known novelist.[226] In 1918, upon his return to Poland after the war, he published a few good books about his adventures in Asian Russia. The titles were: *Kar-Chat, Karapet's Diary, Humanity,* and *From Day to Day.*[227] Later, however, he chose the easy way. He became an official poet laureate and received substantial government grants. His style deteriorated, he traveled extensively at government expense to Egypt, India, and Iceland, and wrote quite mediocre reports. Later, during the period of OZN,[228] he deteriorated even more. He became a semi-official eulogist of totalitarianism and fascism. He joined the ranks of some Poles of German extraction, like Mosdorf,[229] Stahl,[230] etc., who with the zeal of neophytes cultivated nationalism and

---

226 Ferdynand [Ferdek] Goetel (1890–1960), a Polish writer, playwright, journalist, scenarist, and politician, president of the Polish PEN Club in 1926–1933, member of the Polish Academy of Literature from 1935. Goetel spent World War II in Warsaw. In 1943, he took part in uncovering mass graves of Polish officers in Katyń on behalf of the Polish Red Cross, and in this connection testified at US Congress hearings in 1951–1952.

227 Ferdynand Goetel, *Kar-Chat* (1922); *Pątnik Karapeta* (1921); *Ludzkość* (1925); *Z dnia na dzień* (1926).

228 Obóz Zjednoczenia Narodowego ("Camp of National Unity," abbreviated OZN, and often called Ozon, Polish for "ozone"), a Polish political party founded in 1937 by leaders of the Sanation Movement.

229 Jan Mosdorf (1904–1943), a Polish right-wing politician, director of the nationalist organization All-Polish Youth (Młodziez Wszechpolska) and member of the far-right political party Obóz Narodowo-Radykalny (ONR). He also worked as a publicist, under the pseudonym Andrzej Witkowski. Mosdorf died in the Auschwitz concentration camp in 1943, killed for helping Jews.

230 Zdzisław Stahl (1901–1987), a Polish journalist, author of *Zbrodnia Katyńska w świetle dokumentów* (London: "Gryf," 1950), and politician, a member of the Polish Sejm in 1930–1935 and 1938–1939.

extreme antisemitism. By persecuting Jews as intruders, they were underscoring their own "Polishness." At the time of this writing, under German occupation, he all of a sudden remembered his German origins and declared himself a "Volksdeutsch"[231] serving the occupation government.[232]

At the time when I met him, he was still a young boy, eager and full of enthusiasm. When I was thirteen, he became my good friend and introduced me to the secret patriotic organization Promień.[233]

The movement for independence branched off in two directions. One part of the youth congregated under the leadership of Dmowski,[234] with their magazine *Teka*.[235] They preached "national egoism." They were programmed against Germans, Ukrainians, and Jews. They considered a pact with Russia. From this faction originated the founders of the Polish National-Democratic Party and later the Radical Nationalist Party and Falanga.[236] The followers of Promień closely pursued the ideology of the PPS[237] and their aim was to instill in the masses the ideal of Polish independence. Hence, their patriotism was closely linked with the idea of social reforms. I remember the words of the proclamation, which was printed clandestinely, while in the part of Poland under Russian occupation the Polish schools went on strike. It is characteristic how in this proclamation patriotism is combined with radical socialism. The first words of the proclamation were more or less as follows:

> Comrades! Is our blood always to flow with impunity? Do invaders always have to step on our soil? The horrendous, vile prevalence

---

231 Germans by provenance had special privileges under the Nazi regime. No decent person would take advantage of this privilege [J.G.].

232 See discussion in the pre-war press: Ferdynand Goetel, "Dyskusja nad problemem żydowskim w Polsce," *Polityka* 15/161 (10 July 1938): 4–6; Artur Lilien-Brzozdowiecki, "Myśli polskiego Żyda," *Polityka* 18/163 (10 August 1938): 6, 8. See Appendix.

233 "Ray of light" [J.G.].

234 Roman Stanisław Dmowski (1864–1939), a Polish politician, statesman, and chief ideologist and co-founder of the National Democracy ("Endecja") political camp.

235 "Portfolio" [J.G.].

236 All these associations were radically nationalistic and antisemitic [J.G.]. The Falanga faction of the National Radicals (named after Franco's Falange Party), headed by Bolesław Piasecki (1915–1979), embraced fascist terror and violence.

237 The Polish Socialist Party (Polska Partia Socjalistyczna, PPS) was one of the most important Polish left-wing political parties from its inception in 1892 until 1948. It was established again in 1987 and remains active.

of the Russian Empire oppresses us, smothers our national endeavors. Our bishops, plutocracy, and nobility bow to the invaders and let the national flag fall from their weather-beaten hands. Nevertheless the strong grip of the Polish people catches it and proudly hails it again. In them, Poland has not yet perished.

We did not know at that time that this was Józef Piłsudski's doctrine.[238] The head of the circle to which I belonged was comrade Kot, who today is a state minister.[239] We read Darwin, Tylor's *Anthropology*,[240] Engels,[241] and Kautsky.[242] We could have done all this openly, but the romanticism of conspiracy attracted us. For some time the circle was headed by comrade Kukiel, today a general and minister of national defense.[243] We liked him. I cannot forget when, on a November night, during a snow storm, he led us to the cemetery of the insurgents of 1863. Over the graves he gave a fiery speech which he ended as follows:

"We vow . . ."

---

238 Józef Klemens Piłsudski (1867–1935), a Polish statesman. Born under Russian imperial rule to a Polish noble family, he shortly studied medicine, became involved in the revolutionary movement, and was exiled to Siberia. In 1893 he joined Polish Socialist Party (PPS), becoming its leader in 1895. He fled to Galicia in 1901 and traveled to Japan to secure its support for the cause of Polish independence in the wake of the Russo-Japanese War. He formed a paramilitary unit to fight the Russian authorities in 1904 and played a key role in the revolutionary events of 1905 in Congress Poland. In 1906, Piłsudski, with the connivance of the Austrian authorities, organized the nucleus of a future Polish Army. In 1912 he became commander-in-chief of a Riflemen's Association (Związek Strzelecki), and on the outbreak of the First World War he formally established Polish Legions. On 11 November 1918, Piłsudski was appointed commander-in-chief of the Polish forces and was entrusted with creating a national government for the newly independent country. He was a chief of state (1918–1922), "First Marshal of Poland" (from 1920), and *de facto* dictator (1926–1935) of the Second Polish Republic.

239 Stanisław Kot (1885–1975), a Polish historian and politician, member of the Polish Government in Exile, minister of state in the Middle East in 1942–43.

240 Sir Edward Burnett Tylor (1832–1917), an English anthropologist.

241 Friedrich Engels (1820–1895), a German social scientist, author, political theorist, philosopher, and father of communist theory, together with Karl Marx.

242 Karl Kautsky (1854–1938), a Czech-German philosopher and politician. He was a leading theoretician of Marxism. He became the leading promulgator of orthodox Marxism after the death of Friedrich Engels.

243 Marian Włodzimierz Kukiel, who used the pseudonyms Marek Kąkol and Stach Zawierucha (1885–1972), a Polish general, historian, and social and political activist.

We raised our arms in oath and repeated after him: "Therefore we vow not to cease our efforts, to give the last drop of blood, our last breath, until we see our country free and independent."

The revolution was boiling across the borders. In Lwów, some strange new characters appeared. From time to time comrade Józef Piłsudski, then unknown to any of us, came to our meetings. He had the reputation of being an eccentric. He was passionately studying war tactics and strategy. Only later did we learn that in fact he was the very soul of our meetings. Occasionally he stayed at the home of my uncle Rafał Buber[244] on Kraszewskiego Street,[245] where several other conspirators also found hospitality. Allegedly, Trotsky[246] too once lived there, and at another time Feliks Kon, who later became the slaughterer of Kiev. [247]

I was fourteen years old when I sold my stamp collection in order to buy revolvers for the students in Russian Poland. I received the large sum of 1,000 crowns for the album, for which I was able to get twenty Browning pistols. I decided to smuggle them across the border myself. Mr. Jodko-Narkiewicz, the president of PPS, lived with us temporarily at the time and my father suggested that I had better give the arms to him, to assure that they got to the proper hands. I was disappointed and resisted because I was tempted by this adventure, but finally I agreed.

We often demonstrated in the streets; we broke windows of the Russian Consulate; we had bloodless encounters with the police. Once, I was arrested. They took me to the police station, but somehow immediately released me. There was rejoicing when the Japanese defeated

---

244 Rafał Buber, born in 1866, son of Moses and Marie (Lviv PSA AGAD Births 1863–1876, 1900–1901). Rafał Buber was married to Rebeka Bernstein and had one son, Bronisław Julian (b. 1892). Dr. Rafał Buber was a lawyer, a partner of Klemens Sokal (see above). See: *Skorowidz adresowy król. stoł. miasta Lwowa. Rocznik 2. Rok 1910* (Lwów: Jan Rudolf Spigel, 1910), 142. Rafał's father, Moses, was a brother of Salomon Buber (1827–1906), the grandfather of philosopher Martin Buber (1878–1965).

245 Presently Krushelnyts'koi Street.

246 Leon Trotsky (Lev Davidovich Trotsky, 1879–1940), born Lev Davidovich Bronstein, a Bolshevik revolutionary and Marxist theorist.

247 Feliks Yakovlevich Kon (1864–1941), a Polish and Soviet Communist activist. His alleged activity as "the slaughterer of Kiev" is unknown from other sources.

Russia at Tsushima. Inspired by my fantasy, I went to Consul Pustoshkin[248] and offered him one cent toward the rebuilding of the Russian fleet. He accepted it with dignity, but lodged a complaint with Governor Potocki[249] who, in order to give satisfaction to the "friendly power," ordered that I be expelled from all high schools in the Austro-Hungarian Empire.

For a few years I had to study at home and passed examinations every semester. I had excellent teachers. Dr. Józef Reinhold,[250] later professor at the Jagiellonian University [in Kraków], directed my studies while living with us. Besides the required school program, I was taught languages and art, I played the piano, and twice a week Prof. Taubes[251] came to teach me Judaism and Hebrew. At the same time, I was very keen on sports: skiing during the winter, tennis and swimming in the summer, horse riding all year round. In 1906 I won a gold medal in a tennis tournament in Lwów.

I was only twelve years old when Mrs. Helena Szajnocha came to Lwów.[252] She had divorced her husband, the famous geology professor in Kraków and son of Karol Szajnocha.[253] She originated from the Austrian nobility who were sent to Poland with the aim of Germanizing the Poles, and in fact they became completely Polonized instead.

---

248 Konstantin Pavlovich Pustoshkin (1859–1922), consul of the Russian Empire in Naples, Brody, and Lwów.

249 Graf Andrzej Kazimierz Potocki (1861–1908), governor of Galicia in 1903–1908.

250 Józef Reinhold (1884–1928) studied at the universities of Lwów, Vienna, and Berlin and was an extraordinary professor of criminal law at the Jagiellonian University of Kraków in 1921–1928.

251 Probably Zygmunt Taubes, a schoolteacher. See *Księga adresowa Król. Stoł. Miasta Lwowa. Rocznik 17, 1913*, 425.

252 Helena Szajnocha née von Schenk (1864, Stanisławów–1946, Tarnobrzeg), an educator. Szajnocha was also a teacher of an outstanding Austrian writer, Joseph Roth (1894–1939), and of the Polish writer, poet, and translator Józef Wittlin (1896–1976). I am profoundly grateful to Dr. Victoria Lunzer-Talos and Dr. Heinz Lunzer for vast information on Helena Szajnocha and her milieu.

253 Karol Szajnocha (1818–1868), a Polish writer, historian, and independence activist. Self-educated, he nevertheless became a noted Polish historian of the partition period. His son Władysław Szajnocha (1857–1928) was a Polish geologist and pale- ontologist. Since 1885 he lived in Kraków, being a professor at the Jagiellonian University and from 1886 the director of its Geological Cabinet, later the chair of geology; in 1911–1912 and 1916–1917 he served as rector of the Jagiellonian University.

Helena Szajnocha in her room at 7 Hofmana Street in Lwów, 1924.
Courtesy of Leo Baeck Institute, New York

Her father, Baron Schenk, used to be the president of the Court of Appeals in Lwów.[254] Her brother, Józef, called "Pepi,"[255] married Miss Łukasiewicz.[256] He was a judge and later minister of justice in Vienna. Her younger brother, Ernest, was a captain and then a colonel in the cavalry and transferred to the Polish Army after 1918.[257] Ernest was a schoolmate and a good friend of my father.

Mrs. Helena represented the highest degree of European culture. She was highly educated. Her judgment was positive, her taste refined,

---

254 Dr. Josef Eduard Freiherr von Schenk (1813–1891), a jurist, president of the Ober-landesgerichtes (Higher Regional Court) in Lwów in 1872; see R. Harlfinger, "Schenk Josef Eduard Frh. von," in *Österreichisches Biographisches Lexikon*, vol. 10 (Vienna: Verlag der Österreichischen Akademie der Wissenschaften, 1990), 78–79.

255 Josef Wilhelm Freiherr von Schenk (1858–1944), a jurist, minister of justice of the Austro-Hungarian Monarchy in 1916–1917; see H. Karigl, "Schenk Josef Wilhelm Frh. von," in ibid., 79.

256 Valerie Łukasiewicz (1871–1960).

257 Ernst Karl Freiherr von Schenk (1900–1974).

her mind sound. She had a broad field of interests and was an excellent conversationalist. In addition, she possessed good self-control. Her manner was gentle and her will inflexible. She had the charm of the "ancien régime."

One day she complained to my father that she was not active enough. Father advised her to begin giving lessons. Thus, I became her first student. In time, the crowd of her followers grew. Till the end, when I left her in Lwów during World War II, she was an old lady still surrounded by young admirers.[258]

The lessons consisted of my reading aloud in French, sometimes in German, and thoroughly discussing all the topics. In that manner we went over many of the most important works of world literature. Between my twelfth and eighteenth years of age, I spent several hours daily with her. We discussed in depth Goethe's *Faust* with all commentaries; we read French classics, and studied Taine. At home I had to read and write about Dante, Cervantes, Shakespeare, and Carlyle.

The atmosphere surrounding Mrs. Helena was a far cry from nationalist. Her personal origins were deeply rooted in the eighteenth-century Viennese court, when the common language of the civilized world was French. At her parents' home, she was inspired by the times of Metternich,[259] when the vulgarly budding nationalistic movements were distrusted and disdained and attracted only those who were looking for jobs through subversion, and when the military sang in the rhythm of a march:

"Patriot, schlag ihn tot!"[260]

Mrs. Helena could not answer—and did not care—whether she was Polish or German. She was a European of the highest class. In her modest apartment you could feel the atmosphere of old courts.

---

258 I also came to Mrs. Szajnocha a few times a week for French lessons. I was very interested and enjoyed the time spent with this great lady [J.G.].

259 Prince Klemens Wenzel Metternich (1773–1859), a conservative politician, statesman, and diplomat, and state chancellor of Austria who was dismissed during the revolution of 1848.

260 "Beat the patriot to death."

I became fanatically attached to her. She became my guide and confessor. I am sure that I owe her at least half of what I know and what I am.

At this time, when the Communists occupied Lwów in 1939 and while they were still friendly with the Germans, the German ambassador in Moscow, Count Schulenburg,[261] suddenly remembered his kinship with the Schenks and invited them to his estate in Germany. Ernest and his daughters accepted, but the eighty-four-year old Helena sent her reply saying that she had spent all her life in this country [Poland—J. G.] and wanted to share its fate.

After making this heroic decision, she moved in with my cousin Olga on Tarnowskiego Street.[262] It would be a miracle if I were to see her again.

It must have been under her influence that the revolutionary ideas of my youth slowly began to quiet down. Previously, it was mainly the idea of freedom that sparked my fantasy. Now I started to understand the meaning of order and the difficulty of finding the balance between the two of them.

From among the circles of Promień emerged a group of extremists. Some of them even later joined the ranks of the Communists. They wanted to enlist me; they visited me and invited me to their meetings. From time to time, someone stole something from my house and then shamelessly confessed to it. Once they tried to explain to me the necessity of destroying everything that exists in order to build a new world on the old ruins. I could not become convinced. I deeply felt human misfortune and passionately wanted to reform the world. I even thought that I had the know-how to accomplish it. However, instinctively I felt that it was more appropriate to follow the path of gradual reconstruction and reform than that of destruction. It was suggested that I participate in the project to blow up the railroad bridge crossing over

---

261 Friedrich-Werner Graf von der Schulenburg (1875–1944), a German diplomat who served as the last German ambassador to the Soviet Union before Operation Barbarossa. He began his diplomatic career before the First World War, serving as consul and ambassador in several countries.
262 Presently Henerala Tarnavs'koho Street.

Henryk Kolischer, 1920s. *Courtesy of Lviv Historical Museum*

Zamarstynowska Street.[263] Indignantly, I refused. Why? Indeed, this bridge was useful to people.

From time to time I visited the Kolischers in Czerlany.[264] They had a beautiful manor and a paper factory. Often, after breakfast, Uncle Henryk took me for a walk through the park, lecturing me about political economy. "Listen attentively; you will one day be learning it from professors who never in their life saw a bull or a machine. While I not only read many books on the subject, but also am living among bulls and machines. Also, in the parliaments I deal mainly with this subject." Then, in a way that could be understood by a young boy, followed a lecture about the theory of value, lease of land, interest rates, or currency. I was so enthusiastic about the subject that I translated a German economy textbook into Polish.

Thus, I was gradually becoming a conservative.

---

263 Prezently Zamarstynivs'ka Street.
264 Presently Cherlyany in Lviv oblast, Ukraine.

As a result of my father's intensive endeavors, I was admitted to the eighth grade of a public high school.[265] I graduated with honors in 1908 and spent the summer vacation after graduation roaming alone through Norway and sailing the Arctic Ocean. I dreamed and wrote poetry.

∽ ∽ ∽

In autumn of 1908, when I was eighteen years old, I volunteered and joined the 11th Division of Mounted Artillery in Lwów. I liked military service. I made a good impression; I was lively, young, and happy. I was well liked and had excellent horses. In the spring of 1909, I won the first prize in a race of volunteers on their own horses. My Vinea was a beautiful chestnut horse with a proud pedigree. Her father, also named Vinea, won the Derby in Vienna, and her mother Zivatar, after Nonius, came from the emperor's stables in Kisber. From my other mare, Burza,[266] I raised by myself Amurat III (son of Amurat II from the imperial stables in Drohowyż),[267] who later won several prizes on various race tracks.

I advanced quickly; I volunteered for summer exercises and maneuvers and soon became a second lieutenant in the reserves.

After a year of army service, I enrolled in the Department of Law at the University of Lwów. Like many other students, I did not attend the lectures and passed the exams after short periods of intensive study with a private tutor. I took the final exams in Lwów and some state examinations at the University of Vienna. This procedure lasted several years because the First World War interfered. This was the reason why I passed my final exam only in 1916 or 1917 at the University of Lwów, where I received my doctorate in law. Simultaneously, while studying law, I also completed in the same manner a year of the Export Academy in Vienna and gained experience working at my father's bank, as well as the Union Bank in Vienna and Trieste, and participated in the military exercises during the initial years of the war. In 1910, in order to win a

---

265 Senior grade in Polish high schools [J.G.].
266 "Storm" [J.G.].
267 Presently Drohovyzh in Lviv oblast, Ukraine.

bet, I went on an interesting adventure in Greece, almost without money.

One day in 1912, in the street in Lwów, I met Józef Piłsudski. He stopped me and said: "Listen to me, Lilien. You are some kind of an Austrian artillery officer. Maybe you could teach some artillery to my soldiers."

I organized a course, which took place at Kadecka Street.[268] There were thirty-six students in attendance, among them some who later played a prominent role in the revived Poland. The oldest in my class was Kazimierz Sosnkowski, who later became minister of war and is recently commander-in-chief of the Polish Army.[269] It is strange to think that at that time he stood at attention before me, reporting all those present. Among my students was also Marian Kukiel, my old acquaintance from Promień and presently a general and minister of defense.[270] There were also future generals Trojanowski,[271] Zulauf[272] and Nowak;[273] Colonels Krasicki,[274] Dzwonkowski,[275] and more.

My course was later described in the official *Przegląd Artyleryjski*[276] of 1932–1933, in the article entitled "Materials Referring to the History of Artillery of the Polish Legion," where the following sentence appears: "The honorable credit as first executor of orders (of Józef Piłsudski) leading to the creation of the artillery before the First World War, goes to Artur Lilien-Brzozdowiecki, member of the organization Lwowski

---

268 Presently Heroiv Maidanu Street.
269 Kazimierz Sosnkowski (1885–1969, Arundel), a Polish independence fighter, politician, and Polish Army general. He was the creator of the First International Prohibition against Usage of Bacteriological Weapons. He was appointed commander-in-chief of the Polish Army on 8 July 1943.
270 See above, note 243.
271 Mieczysław Ryś-Trojanowski (1881–1945, Mauthausen), a Polish officer, brigadier general of the Polish Army.
272 Juliusz Zulauf (1891–1943, Murnau), a Polish officer, brigadier general of the Polish Army.
273 Karol Ignacy Nowak (1889–1959, London), lieutenant in the 1st Brigade of Polish Light Artillery, later colonel, the commander of the 6th Artillery Group.
274 Mikołaj Freund-Krasicki (1888–1940, Kharkov), a Polish colonel.
275 Zygmunt Michał Ludwik Dzwonkowski (1889–1987, Hamilton), an engineer and infantry colonel in the Polish Army.
276 "Artillery Review" [J.G.].

Strzelec[277] and officer in reserves of the Austrian division of Mounted Artillery stationed in Lwów."[278]

Included in this article there is also a copy of my description of this course as follows:

> To conclude this course, I succeeded in preparing a surprise for my students. I obtained permission from my Division of Mounted Artillery to have my soldiers train with real cannons. I report to say that I was ashamed to lead this division of civilians through the town, while I was in uniform. I did not realize at the time the important historical role these men were to play in the future. Thus I took the streetcar to the barracks and let Sosnkowski lead the men through the city. Many years later, Sosnkowski told me jokingly that that was the day when the modern Polish Army had met for the first time with a real cannon.[279]

Many years later they remembered these days of my activity when in 1927 I was called for maneuvers of the 12th Regiment of Light Cavalry. My commander was my former student, Karol Nowak; that's when I received the medal of distinction, the "Cross of the Legion," personally certified by Marshal Piłsudski. Later I also received the Medal of Poland's Independence.

In 1911, my father died. Our bank was taken over by the Union Bank of Vienna and I became the secretary of the branch in Lwów. I was twenty-one years old when for the first time I felt the weight of responsibility.

I was married in 1913.[280] I was twenty-three years old and my wife was eighteen. For our honeymoon we went to Albania because my wife wanted to see a real war. Poor soul, she saw too much of it later on.

---

277 "Soldier of Lwów" [J.G.].

278 Maksymilian Landau, "Materiały do historji artylerji Legjonów Polskich," *Przegląd artyleryjski* (February 1933): 125.

279 Idem, "Materiały," *Przegląd artyleryjski* (March 1933): 266. Landau quotes from Artur Lilien-Brzozdowiecki, "Garść wspomnień," *Słowo polskie* 169 (21 June 1931): 13.

280 Artur Lilien married Anna Abranowicz (1895, Lwów–1974, New York).

Artur Lilien with his wife Anna, 1913. *Courtesy of Catherine Grun*

In 1914, my son was born. I remember how my beloved wife was leaning over his cradle on the patio at Zofiówka. It was quiet, the linden tree was in bloom, and the bees were buzzing. From the fields I heard the sound of a shepherd's flute; I recorded deep in my memory this sweet melancholic improvisation:

It remained as a symbol of the last idyllic old good times of peace, harmony, security, and carefree days. When I hear this melody I sigh and remember the words of Talleyrand: "Celui qui n'a pas connu l'ancien régime, ne sait pas ce que ça veut dire la joie de vivre."[281]

∽∽ ∽∽ ∽∽

When Archduke Franz Ferdinand was murdered in Sarajevo, I was sure that war was unavoidable. My friends thought I was foolish when I ordered new saddles and uniforms, when I exchanged valuable papers for gold and Swiss francs and paid for all ahead of time, buying at the same time sleeping car tickets to Vienna for my wife and son, valid for travel on the first day of mobilization. In fact, when the war broke out my wife left comfortably with a metal box of valuables, while other ladies were pushing in panic into crowded freight trains.

I reported to my squadron, which was assigned to the 4th Cavalry Division. I enthusiastically went to war against Russia.

On 21 August 1914, I participated in the battle of Jarosławice. There are two books describing this battle: one written by Colonel Grobicki,[282] and the other by Generals Hoen and Waldstätten.[283] The latter very pretentiously describes our defeat as if it were a victory, and my name is mentioned therein. In fact, we lost all our guns while fleeing from a cavalry attack. At one moment I was able to save one cannon, which subsequently got stuck in the mud and fell into Russian hands. Nevertheless I received a decoration *Signum Laudis*.

On 27 September 1914, we again lost some cannons in the battle of Mikuliczyn.[284] I was slightly wounded and, passing through several hospitals, I found myself in Vienna with my family.

---

281 "Whoever has not known the 'old regime' does not know the joy of living" [J.G.]. The exact quote is: "Qui n'a pas vécu dans les années voisines de 1789 ne sait pas ce que c'est que le plaisir de vivre" ("Whoever did not live in the years neighboring on 1789 does not know what the pleasure of living means"). Talleyrand said this to Guizot; quoted in François Pierre Guillaume Guizot, *Mémoires pour servir à l'histoire de mon temps*, 8 vols. (Paris: Levy, 1858–1867), 1:6.

282 Jerzy Grobicki, *Bitwa konna pod Jarosławicami 21 sierpnia 1914 roku* (Warsaw: Wojskowe Biuro Historyczne, 1930).

283 Max von Hoen and Egon Waldstätten, *Die letzte Reiterschlacht der Weltgeschichte: Jaroslawice 1914* (Zurich: Amalthea-Verlag, 1929).

284 Presently Mykulychyn in Ivano-Frankivs'k oblast, Ukraine.

When I was already able to go out, I met in a cafe a relative of my mother, the well-known historian Prof. Szymon Askenazy. He was sitting with a gentleman whom I recognized as Henryk Sienkiewicz.[285] They had arrived from Warsaw via Sweden and were on their way to Switzerland where, later on, they were active in politics.

They invited me to their table. Interested in the opinions among the youth, they asked me what I thought of the war. Without hesitation, I expressed all my anti-Russian feelings and fervently defended the Austro-Polish idea that Poland become an equal partner in the Habsburg Monarchy. To my great astonishment, they shook their heads and Askenazy answered:

"If the Central Powers win, Poland will be independent, but not free. If Russia wins, Poland will be united, but not independent."

"Therefore, what should we wish for?" I asked.

To this, Sienkiewicz gave an answer which at the time seemed to me absurd, but later proved to be prophetic:

"The Central Powers need to defeat Russia and then, in turn, be defeated by the Western Coalition."[286]

For some time afterward, I remained with the staff at Balatonfő-kajár. My wife and son were with me. The little boy made his first steps before my eyes. Later I rode a horse with him sitting in front of me.

From there, I was sent to the front in Carinthia, where I spent two years, surrounded by beautiful mountains, participating more in sports than in fighting. In 1916, I won a difficult hunters' race, "Hubertusritt im Felde,"[287] on my own horse, Naprzód.[288]

A few months later I was again sent to the staff in a beautiful place called St. Andrä im Lavanttal. I rented a lovely hunter's cabin and again brought my family.

Subsequently, I was sent to the front on the river Isonzo and was slightly wounded for the second time. Later, I was on the staff of Gen.

---

285 Henryk Adam Aleksander Pius Sienkiewicz (1846–1916), a Polish journalist and Nobel Prize-winning novelist.
286 That was also Piłsudski's prediction. Cf. Joseph Rothschild, *East Central Europe between the Two World Wars* (Seattle: University of Washington Press, 1974), 45.
287 "Hubertus' Field Race."
288 "Forward" [J.G.].

Boroević[289] in Udine, and finally was assigned to Grado.[290] I had under my command battalions of soldiers and prisoners of war. My duty was to find ammunition sunk by Italians in the lagoons, load it on ships, and deliver it to Trieste. Besides this, I also often served as an artillery observer for the local squadron of sea planes and often flew in front of the enemy, without particular trouble.

Suddenly, in August 1918, I was recalled and, without any effort on my part, I was assigned to our own glass factory in Żółkiew, which at the time was requisitioned by the army and called "K. u. K. Glasfabrik der 4-ten Quartiermeister Abteilung."[291]

This was the end of the First World War for me. I advanced, received a few medals, and mingled with interesting people, even among Imperial Court circles. I had good horses and was cheerful. This was the end of my "good old times."

How beautiful were these years! I was young, cheerful, and handsome. I was loved and had everything one could wish for. I look, as if through a kaleidoscope, at good friends, beautiful girlfriends, purebred horses, colorful uniforms, trips to faraway lands, races, tennis matches, dances, and flowers. And when I dream of those past things, I remember this old little lady of *La Belle aventure*[292] who said with all conviction that the best king of France was Louis Philippe, because she then was sixteen years old.

∽∾ ∽∾ ∽∾

I was in Żółkiew when the war ended. On 1 November, I got across to Lwów in a horse-drawn carriage. It was the last time that Turczyn, my faithful soldier-servant, accompanied me. This honest Ukrainian peasant from Strzeliska near Bóbrka[293] took leave of me in Lwów and returned home.

The road was full of revolting peasants armed with rifles, dressed in sheepskins, and displaying Ukrainian armbands. Under German

---

289 Svetozar Boroević (or Borojević) von Bojna (1856–1920), an Austro-Hungarian field marshal.
290 On the Adriatic Sea [J.G.].
291 "Imperial and Royal Glass Factory, the 4th Quartermaster's Division" [J.G.].
292 Gaston-Arman de Caillavet, *La Belle aventure: Comédie en trois actes* (Paris, 1914).
293 Presently Strilyshcha near Bibrka in Lviv oblast, Ukraine.

pressure, the defeated Austrian army turned their arms over to Ukrainian hands in order to cause more disturbances to the newly emerging Poland.

When I arrived in Lwów, I saw a yellow and blue Ukrainian flag hanging from the City Hall tower. In the streets, truckloads of Ukrainian soldiers were passing, their rifles directed toward civilian passersby.

Some Jewish organization declared its neutrality in the face of the Polish-Ukrainian conflict. I learned that the Polish National Committee was secretly meeting in the building of the Chamber of Commerce. I went there with the rector of the University of Lwów, Prof. Adolf Beck.[294] We declared that not all Jews are neutral and that we represent those who consider the Polish endeavors as theirs, and we place ourselves at their disposal. We were greeted affectionately and cordially accepted into their circle. Present were Count Alexander Skarbek,[295] Prof. Chłamtacz,[296] Stesłowicz,[297] Adam,[298] Henryk Sawczyński,[299] and many others.

After three weeks of street fighting came succor, and the Ukrainians were pushed out of the city. They were, however, still holding it under siege, firing systematically from three sides. The railway line to the west was cleared. It had been cut several times by the Ukrainians, but in general it remained in Polish hands.

When I saw the Polish Army entering and when the yellow and blue Ukrainian flag was replaced by the red and white Polish flag, which floated on the tower, I decided to join the Army. But when I came out to the street I was shocked at what I saw: drunken soldiers were rolling stolen barrels of vodka out of taverns.

"We are requisitioning these for the famous Polish Army!"

---

294 Adolf Beck (1863–1942), an Austrian and Polish physician and professor of physiology at the University of Lwów.

295 Alexander Wincenty Jan Skarbek, Graf (1874–1922), a doctor, politician, and member of the Galician Diet (1906–1918) and the Austrian State Council (1909–1918).

296 Marceli Chłamtacz (1865–1947), a Polish lawyer, scholar of Roman and Civil Law, and professor at Lwów University.

297 Władysław Stesłowicz. See above, note 157.

298 Colonel Adam Tymoteusz Sawczyński (1892–1975).

299 Jan Henryk Sawczyński (1861–1923), a lawyer and historian.

At Krakowska Street[300] they were throwing bales of fabric out of store windows, distributing them among themselves.

Smoke rose over the Jewish quarter.

I met my attorney, Szenker.[301] Together we went to City Hall to urge Mayor Neuman[302] to intervene with the Polish Headquarters at Grunwaldzka Street.[303] We were received by Capt. Jakubski,[304] the chief of staff of Col. Mączyński.[305] He declared that this was not new to him and he did not intend to take any action. He said: "In the Jewish quarter they were shooting at Polish soldiers, they were pouring boiling water over the patrols, and that's why I ordered the punitive expedition against this part of the city." Later, under pressure from abroad, they used every subterfuge to deny everything. But I heard the above statement with my own ears, and this was enough proof of their guilt.

On my way back, I passed a detachment of soldiers singing while they marched:

Pan generał Roja dał mi to na piśmie,
Że każdego żydka tu cholera ściśnie.
Raz, dwa, trzy, cztery, raz, dwa, trzy.
Pokażże mi pokaż żydka bogatego,
A wycisnę zaraz ja bebechy z niego.
Raz, dwa, trzy, cztery, raz, dwa, trzy.[306]

---

300 Presently Krakivs'ka Street.
301 Probably Dr. Izydor Schenker, a lawyer, living at Mochnackiego 22. See *Księga adresowa Król. Stoł. Miasta Lwowa. Rocznik 17, 1913*, 317.
302 Józef Neumann (1857–1932) was president of the City of Lwów in 1911–1914 and 1919–1927.
303 Presently Gryunval'ds'ka Street.
304 Dr. Antoni Jakubski (1885–1962), a zoologist, took part in the First World War and Polish-Ukrainian battle of Lwów in November 1918.
305 Czesław Mączyński (1881–1935), a Polish officer and politician.
306 "Gen. Roja gave me in writing that every Jew should drop dead./ One, two, three, four, one, two, three./ Bring to me a wealthy Jew and I will squeeze the guts out of him./ One, two, three, four, one, two, three." Bolesław Roja (1876–1940) was an officer of the Polish Legions in the First World War, a general, and a politician in the Second Polish Republic. He was appointed a brigadier general of the Polish Army on 1 November 1918. He opposed Józef Piłsudski and his Sanation regime

Upon returning home, I found a military patrol led by Captain Św. terrorizing my wife with pistols and conducting a "search." They stole a watch from our neighbors but did not take anything from us. I was arrested.

The reason for my arrest was as follows: in the entrance to the building, in accordance with the law, there was a list of tenants. Next to my name displayed my religion as Jewish, nationality Polish. "How dare this dirty Jew pass for a Pole?" I was released immediately when I mentioned the name of my friend Stesłowicz, who at the time was chief of the local temporary government. I saw, however, in that guardhouse how they send away detained culprits, how they arrested the scum and individuals of non-Polish origin; they immediately released the Poles, especially soldiers.

At this moment something happened in me. My country, of which I had dreamed for twenty-eight years of my life, all of a sudden became a reality and greeted me with the glare of Jewish pogroms.

Until now, I had always lived in the atmosphere of western civilization. Suddenly and unexpectedly a monstrous wind blew from the East. Something inconceivable. Some fantastic, uncanny scenes, the likes of which you heard happening in half-Asiatic Kishinev,[307] suddenly became a reality magnified a hundred times in my own, nice, intelligent, smiling Lwów. Hundreds and hundreds of corpses; a whole neighborhood in ashes.

I ground my teeth and decided that even if I had to be shot, I would never join *such* an army.

A few days later, Messrs Chrzanowski[308] and Wasserzug[309] arrived on behalf of the Ministry of Foreign Affairs in Warsaw to investigate,

---

after the coup of 1926. After the German invasion of Poland in 1939, he was arrested by the Nazis and died in the Sachsenhausen concentration camp.

307 A great antisemitic pogrom took place in the Moldavian city of Kishinev/Chişinău (then in the Russian Empire) on 6–7 April 1903. The rioting continued for three days, resulting in 47–49 Jews dead, 92 severely wounded, and 500 suffering minor injuries. In addition, several hundred houses and many businesses were plundered and destroyed.

308 Leon Chrzanowski, a diplomat.

309 Józef Wasserzug, a journalist.

to reveal the truth and pinpoint who was responsible. The culprits had incited the improvised army to battle by promising a three-day debauch in the Jewish quarter. And they kept their promise. They spread rumors that 1) the pogroms did not happen at all; 2) that pogroms were incited by the Ukrainians; 3) by released criminals; 4) by the Jewish scum itself. Jews were blamed for daring to complain, for speaking about pogroms at all, thus damaging the image of Poland on the international scene. The culprits were not the ones who committed the crime, but its victims. The one who was murdered was guilty, not the murderer.

When I was summoned to appear at City Hall, I decided to speak openly, notwithstanding the results. I wrote down several facts pointing to the responsibility of the military command. I said everything and set it down in writing. I was ready for the worst. I even prepared myself for the idea that I might be shot.

In the afternoon, however, Chrzanowski and Wasserzug came to see me. They did not seem to want to arrest me. They sat down for tea and Chrzanowski said:

"What you have told us is appalling. It's like an abyss is opening which will swallow both the Jews and the Poles in a common grave. We must build bridges over this precipice. The bridge will consist of our collaboration and we came to ask you to go with us to Warsaw and work for the Ministry of Foreign Affairs."

I was so touched that I couldn't control myself and burst into tears like a child. At last, my beloved country extended her hand to me over the still smoldering ashes.

I went. I could not join the army as I was too badly hurt. I began, however, to work eagerly with the Ministry of Foreign Affairs. I was appointed to the Bureau of Congressional Work, which prepared speeches for the Polish delegation in Versailles.

Still, I did not become their regular employee because, in general, they resented people who came from formerly Austrian Poland. Those educated under Russian rule set the tone. Many of them were educated only by tutors, without higher education. They envied those whom they sarcastically called "the import from Galicia" and constantly interfered with their work. I was asked to write only two papers on economy and I wrote about "The Actual Situation of the Banks in Poland" and "The Basis of the Future Polish Currency." Then my work discontinued.

My wife and son were with me in Warsaw. I unsuccessfully looked for work and in the meantime had to live on checks drawn on the bank in Lwów. Suddenly the bank closed during the siege of Lwów and one of my checks returned unpaid. I could not find work and had to make an urgent decision. I went to Vienna and became involved in risky businesses that were prospering in the postwar economy. I was successful, brought over my wife and child, and lived independently for a few months. In the meantime, the Ukrainians retreated from Lwów and my mother sent a telegram urging me to return, take care of the family business, and reopen the glass factory.

✎ ✎ ✎

During this time, Poland underwent an invisible revolution. Power was taken over by a new class of people—intellectual and semi-intellectual proletarians. The circles representing the old tradition of Polish culture in the midst of whom I was brought up and in which I felt at home were pushed aside and no longer had any influence. The nobility with political know-how and the middle class with higher education who did not belong to the new popular trend—including the leading Jewish intelligentsia—were all pushed out of their positions. Only in rare cases were they allowed to perform duties requiring high qualifications, but as a rule they were restricted to secondary positions.

New people took over the leading positions. They set the tone and created new criteria in ideas and behavior. The old experience in the art of ruling was considered out of style. The law was derided. The newcomers were convinced that where there was a will, there was a way; that if you threw a person into deep water, he would be able to swim. They seized the remnants of the ruined national economy and proudly declared: "We don't need your approval, since the days of appealing to your hearts and purses are over." Now "authority" replaced "appealing."

They came from nowhere. In the past they had been good citizens and fought valiantly for the freedom of their country. Now they proclaimed that in return they deserved to be their country's masters: all the others were to them "economic circles which inherited Poland for free." Despite their initial idealism, it ultimately turned out that they never fought for Poland's independence and were here "for free." Because when they came to power, all internal, personal, and economic politics were aimed at consolidating the power and wellbeing of this new ruling class. They filled all important military and administrative posts. Industry, commerce, and finance were manned by "their people." They acquired wealth, mansions, and automobiles and lived in opulence. And so, comfortably relaxed, they found the new situation "great."[310]

Anyone who would dare criticize would be a threat to this bliss. He would be considered a traitor and the reprisals against such people were most severe, from banishment up to Bereza Kartuska.[311] From the very beginning, people whose fathers meant anything at all in the old regime were looked upon with suspicion.

As far as the Jews were concerned, they were not looked upon as normal citizens but rather as uninvited guests and unwillingly tolerated intruders. They were oppressed, often beaten. Such behavior was tolerated with indulgence. If the oppressed dared to complain or fought back, this was met with indignation. In the old times, too, there were antisemitic brawls—even in Lwów. They were usually organized by students from boarding schools, living on charity. In such instances, Jews turned for protection to the *voivod* (governor), castellan, or *starost* (a crown land administrator), who sent out servants with halberds and soon restored order. But now there were no more descendants of such Mniszechs or Stadnickis,[312] who needed and protected Jews because they understood how useful they were for society. Now absolute power

---

310 *Byczo jest* [S.K.]. Excerpt from a Polish song [J.G.].
311 A jail for political prisoners where they were treated sadistically [J.G.]. The Bereza Kartuska Detention Camp (Miejsce Odosobnienia w Berezie Kartuskiej, "Place of Isolation at Bereza Kartuska") was a Polish place of detention, principally for political prisoners, that operated in 1934–1939 at Bereza Kartuska in the former Polesie Province (today in Belarus, near the city of Brest).
312 Noble Polish families.

was in the hands of the descendants of those seventeenth-century students who found utmost pleasure in this *Schülergeläuf*.[313]

Thus, there were two sets of reasons why I was not successful; I was a gentleman and I was a Jew.

And still I loved Poland. Her landscape was my landscape. Her language was my language, her song was my song, her tradition—my tradition. And Lwów, this beautiful Lwów, my dearest city! The city of gardens among green hills with a hundred noble towers rising toward the sky. The city of my family treasures, where not only cemeteries, but also things alive, public buildings, institutions, and railway lines told me the history of my fathers and forefathers.

I longed to be part of it and share responsibilities, but I found obstacles everywhere. I was further pushed to the margins of true life. Gradually I developed in my soul a *complex of rejected love*.

This complex became prevalent among Polish Jews. In some it evoked an open revolt; in others, utter bitterness, and in those like myself, a feeling of deep sorrow.

I was forced to limit myself to small dealings. I bought out my uncles' shares in Zofiówka and remodeled the house into one large apartment. I loved Zofiówka. I loved every tree which I had climbed as a boy, I loved every pebble, every cloud in the sky. Once I was talking about some beautiful places in the world—Sorrento, the Bosporus, Isola Bella, the Lake of Geneva. Someone asked me where I would make my home if I had to choose. I was very surprised by this question. Of course I would choose the place where my home stands now!

I loved not only my home, but also my old belongings. Some were inherited, some collected by myself. I had the family archives, among them old papers, old letters carefully sorted and yellowed with age, and complete sets of my father's periodical *Ojczyzna*.[314] I had a large library of several thousands of volumes, some of them very rare.

---

313 Literally "a running of pupils," a riot. See Majer Bałaban, *Dzielnica żydowska, jej dzieje i zabytki* (Lwów: Towarzystwo Miłośników Przeszłośći Lwowa, 1909), 34.

314 "Fatherland," here also meaning, Adolf's fatherland. See above, p. 45.

Among them were a complete set of the first edition of the works of Kochanowski,[315] the first edition of *Żywoty świętych* by Skarga,[316] *Podróż na wschód* by Raczyński,[317] the first edition of Luther's Bible,[318] an illustrated Rabelais of 1610,[319] "L'Art de Fortification" by Vauban,[320] old works on astrology, alchemy, travelogues, chivalric codes, dictionaries, court anecdotes, Jesuit manuals for confessors entitled "Casuistica moralis."

Among my collections was one of the six watches which Napoleon I had once ordered as presents. They were described by Maze-Sencier in his book *Les fournisseurs de Napoléon*.[321] It was made of gold covered with dark green enamel, with diamond garlands on both sides and in the middle was a diamond "N" surmounted by a crown. A Napoleon eagle was stamped on the case. Great-grandfather Majer Rachmiel bought it in 1841 at Köchert's in Vienna.[322] I had many other beautiful objects. A Louis XVI snuff box made of four-color gold with a beautiful miniature of a nymph in a garden; large china figures from Sèvres representing Poniatowski, Bernadotte,[323] and Beauharnais;[324] a portrait

---

315 Jan Kochanowski (1530–1584), a Polish Renaissance poet who established poetic patterns that would become integral to the Polish literary language.

316 Piotr Skarga, *Żywoty Swiętych starego y nowego zakonu z pisma świętego y z poważnych pisarzow y Doktorow koscielnych wybranych* [. . .] (Wilno: Mikołaj Krzysztof Radziwiłł, 1579).

317 Probably Edward Raczyński, *Dziennik podróży do Turcyi odbytej w roku 1814* (Wrocław: W.B. Korn, 1823).

318 A German translation of the Bible by Martin Luther, first printed with both Testaments in 1534.

319 Probably, François Rabelais, *La plaisante, et ioyeuse histoyre du grand geant Gargantua*, 3 vols. (Geneva?, ca. 1600).

320 Probably, Sébastien Le Prestre de Vauban et al., *Maniere de fortifier de Mr. de Vauban: Où l'on voit de quelle méthode on se sert aujourd'hui en France, pour la fortification des places tant régulieres qu'irréguliers: En quoi cette méthode differe des autres, &c.: Avec un traité de geometrie qu'on a mis à la tête, pour avoir une parfaite intelligence des fortifications* (Amsterdam, 1689).

321 Alphonse Maze-Sencier, *Les fournisseurs de Napoléon Ier et des deux impératrices* (Paris: H. Laurens, 1893).

322 Jakob Heinrich Köchert (1795–1869), an Austrian jeweler, the founder of the renowned firm A. E. Köchert.

323 Probably Charles XIV and Charles III John, also Carl John (1763–1844), King of Sweden (as Charles XIV John) and King of Norway (as Charles III John) from 1818 until his death, born as Jean Baptiste Jules Bernadotte.

324 Eugène Rose de Beauharnais (1781–1824), an adopted son of Napoleon I; see Tamara Préaud, "Les Grands Hommes en Sculptures à Sèvres au XIXème siècle,"

of young Prince Adam Czartoryski in a confederate uniform;[325] fifteenth-century spoons from Gdańsk; good old furniture, and rare carpets. Later, when times became difficult, I was obliged to gradually sell some of those treasures. However, quite a few were still left as prey for invaders.

I gradually recovered from the shock of the pogroms. I was trying to reason that this "army" was created in the period of postwar chaos— improvised out of an underground gang—and that anything could happen during the frenzy of war. I realized that, after all, there was a time when this improvised army was the only somehow organized armed force between the Rhine and Kamchatka.

Miłość tak pięknie tłomaczy
Kłamstwo i zdradę i grzech . . .[326]

I decided to bury the memory of the pogroms. I joined the army and became a reserve lieutenant of the 12th Regiment of Light Artillery.

When I belonged to Strzelec, I often used the pseudonym "Brzozdowiecki" in memory of Brzozdowce, the town from where the Lilien family came. I also sometimes wrote under this name. Now, a new law allowed to add the pseudonyms assumed during service in the [Polish] Legion to the family surname, and thus I became Lilien-Brzozdowiecki.[327]

On New Year's Day of 1921, my dearest daughter was born. She could hardly talk when she gave herself the name Ajusia.[328] Since then, for me,

---

The French Porcelain Society Journal 2 (2005): 120–132.

325 Prince Adam Kazimierz Czartoryski (1734–1823), a Polish nobleman, statesman, traveler, and author. He was the marshal of the General Confederation of the Kingdom of Poland (1812–1813), established by Emperor Napoleon in Poland on the eve of his campaign in Russia.

326 "Love can excuse so well/ lies, betrayal and sin . . ." Words of a Polish song [J.G.]. The song *Miłość ci wszystko wybaczy* (Love will excuse everything) was written by poet Julian Tuwim under the pseudonym Oldlen and composer Henryk Wars for the film *Szpieg w masce* (Spy in a Mask, 1933); it was performed by Hanka Ordonówna and became a hit.

327 Lilien-Brzozdowiecki became Artur Lilien's official name in 1929; see *Gazeta Lwowska*, 10 December 1929.

328 Joanna [J.G.].

this will always be her name. Shortly after her arrival, I became estranged from my dear wife. She was beautiful and I loved her very much.

My mother took care of my little daughter, and my good cousin Olga brought her up. Ajusia was sweet, good, and gentle. She was filled with a great love, which embraced everything. She loved and understood animals and they in turn loved and understood her. When she was still very young, she tamed a squirrel and called it Śmiguś.[329] All day Śmiguś ran free in the woods and came back at night to sleep under Ajusia's pillow. When she passed the grove, she made some signs and Śmiguś ran to her and sat on her shoulder. One day, on Hala Gąsienicowa,[330] we passed a herd of cows. She saw a calf and started to talk to it and caressed its head. She must have had some magic power, because the calf left its own mother and followed us like a little dog.

I reactivated the glass factory. I became vice-president of my father's bank, now called Bank Unji w Polsce, S.A. we Lwowie. I became a member of the Chamber of Commerce and belonged to the Bankers Association. I wrote articles on economy for *Czas*,[331] published in Kraków, or for *Gazeta Bankowa*.[332]

It was not only my personal status that was now lower than the standards upon which I grew up. Lwów also was not the same anymore. During my youth it was throbbing with creative verve, opulence, and animation. Poetry, literature, science, theater, and art flourished, as did the economy and elegant social life. Now Warsaw took away all the vital force. Life became empty, impoverished, and dead. Nevertheless, the immortal humor of the urchin of Lwów survived, and he sang to the tune of the old beggar's song:

Żebrak za żebrakiem,
Za żebrakiem żebrak,

---

329 "Propeller" [J.G.].
330 In the Tatra Mountains [J.G.].
331 "Time" [J.G.].
332 "Bank Gazette" [J.G.]. See, for instance, Artur Lilien, "Ochrona drobnego akcjonariusza," *Gazeta Bankowa* (25 June 1928): 281–282.

A za tym żebrakiem
Wywiadowcy nie brak.[333]

A brighter spot in this picture were meetings of the Stronnictwo Konserwatywne,[334] of which I became a member. At the Thursday afternoon tea in the apartment of the Paygerts,[335] which was filled with antiques, assembled the remaining elite of the landed gentry, some prominent professors, industrialists, and writers. They wielded no political influence, but someone always gave a lecture, either on an actual problem or on such remote subjects as "The Forestry Politics of Loret," or "Subjectivism in Historiography." The ladies served tea and the discussion evolved on a high level, in a good old fashion.

Once a month someone from out of town came to give a lecture— the president of the party, Prince Janusz Radziwiłł,[336] or some ambassador or senator. Once, Mackiewicz came.[337] He gave me the strange impression of a very intelligent brawler. He was supposed to be a conservative, like ourselves. It made me think, however, that we came from the European school of Bobrzyński,[338] and he probably from the Asiatic school of Purishkevich—father of the Tsarist "Black Hundred."[339]

---

333 "Beggar after beggar,/ after beggar—beggar,/ and after that beggar,/ a secret agent follows" [J.G., S.K.].

334 "Conservative Party" [J.G.].

335 University professor Jan Paygert (1863–1917) lived at 3 Karola Ludwika (later Legionów) Street before the First World War. See *Księga adresowa Król. Stoł. Miasta Lwowa. Rocznik 17, 1913*, 320. That street is presently the western side of Svobody Avenue.

336 Janusz Franciszek Prince Radziwiłł (1880–1967), a Polish nobleman and politician.

337 Probably Stanisław "Cat" Mackiewicz (1896–1966), a Polish conservative writer and monarchist.

338 Michał Hieronim Bobrzyński (1849–1935), a Polish historian, conservative politician, and governor of Galicia.

339 Vladimir Mitrofanovich Purishkevich (1870–1920), a Russian conservative politician. The Black Hundred (Чёрная сотня, *Chornaya sotnya* in Russian) was a counter-revolutionary movement in Russia in the early twentieth century, a supporter of the tsarist regime, which stood for inviolable autocracy in its struggle against the revolutionary movement. It was noted for its extremist nationalism and xenophobia, which included antisemitism, incitement to pogroms, and anti-Ukrainian sentiments.

But in fact, one could still breathe the atmosphere of the good old times only in the company of those conservatives.

When a wave of Russian emigrants came to Poland after the revolution, I hosted many of them in my home. I thought that if the revolution can bring about murder and devastation under the motto "Proletarians of all countries, unite!" one should at least come to the rescue of the survivors under the motto "Gentlemen of all countries, unite!" Besides, I thought, one day I could find myself in a similar situation.

And so, my home gave shelter to a variety of people. With some of them I became friends and succeeded in helping them to build a new life. Colonel Gonczarow was my guest for eight years.[340] There were also some who did not deserve my friendship.

Later, the roomy and deserted Zofiówka often became a refuge for people in need of shelter. For many months, my friend St.[anisław] Czajkowski[341] and his wife lived there when he lost his job; also another friend, Edw.[ard] Skowroński, after he lost his position as consul in Harbin,[342] when these jobs were filled with members of the clique. In his case, they let him go under the pretext that his beautiful wife whom he brought along, was not only German by birth but, moreover, née Bismarck.[343] Later, old Mr. Nossig lived at Zofiówka after fleeing from Hitler. During the last winter, I was hosting two strangers, Jewish engineers, escapees from Berlin. Once before, the satirist Hemar[344] lived in my house when he, a young man, quarreled with his family and needed a roof over his head. During the last summer before the war, my sister

---

340 Probably, Arkadjusz Gończarow (Аркадий Гончаров), who later worked as a manager in the Żółkiew glass factory. See Józef Jakubowski et al., eds., *Rocznik polskiego przemysłu i handlu* (Warsaw: Polska spółka wydawnictw informacyjnych, 1936), no. 3763.

341 Probably Stanisław Czajkowski (1878–1954), a Polish artist.

342 Edward Skowroński served as Polish consul in Harbin from December 1930 to October 1931.

343 Bismarck was the famous Prussian chancellor at the time of the Franco-Prussian war [J.G.].

344 Marian Hemar (1901–1972), born Jan Maria Hescheles, a Polish-Jewish poet, journalist, playwright, and comedy writer. Hemar was a cousin of Polish author Stanisław Lem (1921–2006).

Mania invited the writer Andrzejewski,[345] who wanted to spend a few months wandering in our region.

ఎం ఎం ఎం

The times became increasingly difficult and more and more obstacles were piling up before me. In 1928, the bank changed hands again and I lost my job. I tried to find something in Warsaw. I looked for the support of people who had grown up around my family and took advantage of our support and now reached high positions.

The son of Uncle Kolischer's administrator in Czerlany[346] rose to the rank of general and became the president of the High Chamber of State Control. The playmate of my Löwenstein relatives, who lived with them since childhood, became chief director of the powerful Bank Gospodarstwa Krajowego.[347] The son of the teacher in Czerlany was the second director of this bank. A poor young man who for many years was my companion, ate at our table, and thanks to my father's financial support graduated from the Export Academy in Vienna, was now president of the British-Polish Bank in Gdańsk. One of the clerks who used to work for me in our bank became the director of the Communal Savings Bank in Lwów, another one had become president of the Chamber of Commerce, and still another department head at the Ministry of Commerce and Industry.

Apart from the above-mentioned general, who in fact once proved his friendliness toward me, none of them did anything for me. They avoided me, perhaps because I reminded them of the times when they were still humble. Warsaw did not want me.

Discouraged, I returned home, settled in Żółkiew, and personally took over the management of our glass factory.

There, the family owned a little house. Domesticated deer lived in the garden. Our fields extended down the hill from the Haraj Forest.

---

345 Jerzy Andrzejewski (1909–1983), a prolific Polish author of such popular novels as *Noc* (Night, 1945) and *Popiół i Diament* (Ashes and Diamonds, 1948, adapted into a film by director Andrzej Wajda in 1958).

346 The estate of our relatives, the Kolischers [J.G.].

347 "The State Bank of Poland" [J.G.].

I had horses and a carriage, and a merry horse-drawn sleigh in winter. There were friendly manors in the neighborhood and a club in the town. My good cousin Zośka[348] took care of the household.

Żółkiew itself was teeming with history. Here stood the castle of the great *Hetman*,[349] in front of which was the Town Square surrounded by houses with arcades. This square once belonged to the castle, where squadrons of armored combatants were formed. On each side were old fortress walls and the Glińsko and the Lwów city gates; and atop all, a beautiful parish church decorated with coats of arms of the Żółkiewski, Sobieski, and Daniłowicz families.[350] Leaning against the walls of the citadel was a belfry in Renaissance style. It now stood in venerable silence, but to whoever could hear its voice cried loudly over the ages the very motto for which our old knights lived and died:

"God and Fatherland."

Its bells tolled with devotion and many a shot was fired against the hordes.

Inside the church there were tombs of knights. The inscriptions carved in marble tell stories of their battles against Turks and Tatars, Cossacks and Muscovites. They tell how this or that Sobieski fought

---

348 Zofia Stande née Lilien.

349 Stanisław Żółkiewski (1547–1620), a Polish nobleman, magnate, and military commander who took part in many campaigns both in Poland and on its southern and eastern borders. He held a number of notable posts in the administration of the Polish-Lithuanian Commonwealth, including castellan of Lwów (from 1590), voivod of Kijów, and Great Chancellor of the Crown (from 1618). Following 1588, he was also a Field Crown *Hetman*, in 1613 promoted to Grand *Hetman* of the Crown. During his lifetime he won major military victories against Muscovy, the Ottoman Empire, and the Tatars. He was the first European invader of Russia to seize Moscow, a distinction shared only with Napoleon. *Hetman* was the title of the second highest military commander (after the monarch) in fifteenth- to eighteenth-century Poland and the Grand Duchy of Lithuania.

350 Families of great merit in Poland's history [J.G.]. Stanisław Żółkiewski was the founder of the town of Żółkiew (1597). Stanisław's daughter Zofia (ca. 1594–1634) married Jan Daniłowicz (1570–1628), the voivod of Ruthenia (from 1613). Daniłowicz's grandson Jan Sobieski (1629–1696), the Polish King John III (reigned 1674–1696), inherited the town from his mother, Zofia Teofila née Daniłowiczówna.

the rebels or how young Daniłowicz was taken to Khan Temir's[351] prison and tortured to death.

This heroic paean is very Polish and European at one and the same time. They were all very much aware of the fact that they not only defended the borders of their own country, but at the same time they fought in defense of the great western civilization, while the Polish borders were the bulwark of Christianity. First place among those tombs was the Renaissance tomb of Stanisław Żółkiewski, the foremost Polish hero of all time.

I lived thus in the shadow of *Hetman* Żółkiewski's tomb, and I often thought about this great warrior and statesman.

How he defeated Moscow and conquered the Kremlin.[352]

How the Russian *boyars*[353] asked him to convert to the Orthodox faith and accept their throne, but he promoted instead the heir to the Polish throne, Prince Władyslaw, in his place. How the Jesuits forced King Sigismund to give a reply which filled him with bitterness:

> You talk with Moscow as equals, forgetting that you are the victor. Put your foot down and dictate your conditions instead of bending to their demands and jeopardizing the salvation of the Prince's soul.

I reminisced how this great warrior Żółkiewski suppressed revolts in the country, restoring order, and finally perished in the battle of Cecora,[354] betrayed and abandoned, trying to stop the whole Turkish horde of invaders with only a handful of his heroic men. He was a true seventy-year-old Polish Leonidas. His head, detached from the body,

---

351 Khan Temir (Polish: Kantymir Murza, nicknamed Bloody Sword; died 1637), a powerful khan of the Budjak Nogais (Budjak Horde); around 1603, he formed and subsequently led the Nogai Khanate. Stanisław Daniłowicz, son of Zofia, was captured in battle, tortured to death, and then his body was ransomed.

352 In 1610.

353 A *boyar* (Russian: боярин) was a member of the highest rank of the feudal Moscovian aristocracy, second only to the ruling princes.

354 The Battle of Ţuţora (also known as the Battle of Cecora), between the Polish-Lithuanian Commonwealth and Ottoman forces backed by Nogais, was fought from 17 September to 7 October 1620 in Moldavia, near the Prut River.

was sent as a trophy to Istanbul. It was redeemed eight years later by his widow and laid in the family grave with the following inscription:

Exoriatur Aliquis Nostris Ex Ossibus Ultor.[355]

And from his bones an avenger indeed was born. Jan III Sobieski, who defeated the Turks at Vienna, was a great-grandson of the *Hetman*. Many a memento of this king also remains in Żółkiew. He spent here, at the castle, the first nine years of his life and later frequently visited it. In the parish church there are several tombs of his closest family members and four huge paintings depicting his battles.[356] He donated funds for the Jewish synagogue, which has been in use till the present.[357] Its multi-branched menorahs were adorned with large Polish eagles. Beyond the walls were military caserns occupied 250 years ago by the dragoons of King Jan and recently housing the 6th Regiment of Polish Cavalry.

In my imagination, however, it was the *Hetman* who played the principal role. I felt deeply that this shield defending the Polish borders was simultaneously the shield for our entire civilized world. *Hetman* was a knight of Europe, like Miltiades,[358] like El Cid.[359] Ungrateful Europe could quietly develop behind his back, while he fought and died for her. However, not only did Europe not come to his aid, but did not even preserve the memory of his name. His efforts and his name are forgotten today.

---

355 "May an avenger rise from our bones" [J.G.]. Quotation from Virgilius, *Aeneid*, IV, 625.

356 The parish (collegiate) church of St. Laurence in Żółkiew was built in 1606–1618 by architects Paweł Szczęśliwy (Paolo the Lucky) and Amroży Przychylny (Ambroggio Nutclauss).

357 This synagogue is the so-called Sobieski Shul, built in 1692, probably by architect Peter Beber.

358 Miltiades the Younger (ca. 550–489 BCE) successfully presented himself as a defender of Greek freedoms against Persian despotism. He was elected to serve as one of the ten generals for 490 BCE. He is often credited with devising the tactics that defeated the Persians in the Battle of Marathon later that year.

359 Rodrigo Díaz de Vivar (ca. 1040–1099), known as El Cid Campeador, a Castilian nobleman, military leader, and diplomat who, after being exiled, conquered and governed the city of Valencia. Rodrigo Díaz was educated in the royal court of Castile and became the *alférez*, or chief general, of Alfonso VI, and his most valuable asset in the fight against the Moors.

Thus, he became a symbol of the part Poland played in this world, a symbol of Poland misunderstood by those for whom she bleeds, receiving no help whatsoever in her deadly efforts towards the common good; a symbol of Poland bearing alone on her shoulders the "the white man's burden."[360]

Sometimes I allowed myself some familiarity when thinking of *Hetman* and his royal great-grandson. It was nice to realize that these prominent people probably spoke with the same pleasant melodic accent of Lwów which is my mother tongue. Sometimes I thought of my ancestors, contemporaries of the *Hetman*. During the *Hetman*'s life, Saul arrived in Nieśwież,[361] Michael Lilien appeared in Brzozdowce, and the Golden Rose was conducting a lawsuit with the Jesuits. Independently of him, they all led their modest lives; maybe Saul had met the *Hetman* in the political arena; maybe some time Rose caught a glimpse of him since he often stayed in the neighboring Lwów. In my reflections, it sometimes struck me that the life of His Highness the *Hetman* and those of Saul and Michael and Rose must have intersected somewhere along the way with the Jesuits.

I got to love provincial life and returned to Zofiówka only on weekends. I would have been glad to live this way, if only I saw results from my hard and strenuous labor.

I developed the glass factory and pioneered alone, without any government intervention, the export of our products to Egypt. In 1932, I managed to export 160 railroad carloads of cylinders for petroleum lamps—valued at $80,000 in gold. In 1933, however, I was forced to stop production due to a series of impediments: excessive taxes, governmental chicanery, huge costs required for the inefficient social security, terrible economic mismanagement, and a wave of bankruptcies among our buyers. My funds were exhausted. I sold all the real estate except Zofiówka and the factory. The cash was used up; the debts were growing and an attorney, Dr. Mayer,[362] who recently became our partner, committed suicide.

---

360 An allusion to the poem "The White Man's Burden" by Rudyard Kipling (1899).
361 Presently Nyasvizh in Belarus.
362 Dr. Henryk Mayer or Dr. Aleksander Mayer.

I gave a power of attorney to a lawyer and helped organize a workers' cooperative, which leased and managed the operations. As for myself, I left again for Warsaw to look for employment.

The Department of Foreign Affairs knew of my successes in export. With the support of the general mentioned above, they proposed offering me the position of consul in Alexandria.

Colonel Jaroszewicz,[363] the Polish ambassador in Cairo, opposed it. I learned that Mrs. Pawlewska knew him well. She was a good friend of my mother, now an influential person, a friend of Mrs. Piłsudski, and the mother-in-law of two generals. I asked her to put in a good word with Jaroszewicz on my behalf. She refused. She asked me why I didn't look for a job in Vienna. Once again I felt this allusion to me as a foreigner like a bad slap in the face from my own country. After all, she was a friend of my mother, and as a child I played with her children.

The Department of Foreign Affairs offered me the post of consul in Beirut or Baghdad. I did not see there any real chance to develop exports from Poland. I wanted Egypt because the prospects there were colossal, but much neglected. Finally I agreed to the post of commercial attaché in Tel Aviv.

With a heavy heart I left Poland in June 1934. A group of Jewish *ḥalutzim*[364] was also on board the M/S *Polonia*. When the yellow shores of Palestine appeared on the horizon, they all stepped out onto the deck and solemnly, in chorus, sang the *Hatikvah*;[365] then, forming a circle, they danced the *hora*, their national dance. I watched in amazement and some kind of envy. These people, after thousands of years of wandering, felt that they were returning, that they were approaching something of their own, something for which they were longing.

I felt like an exile, thrown onto strange, barren, inhospitable shores.

Palestine is a child of the pogroms. Were there no physical and moral pogroms in Europe, the actual Palestine would have never been

---

363 Tadeusz Jaroszewicz (1890–1934), a Polish lieutenant-colonel and diplomat.
364 Hebrew: pioneers.
365 *Hatikvah* (Hebrew: The Hope), a Zionist anthem, the national anthem of Israel from 1948.

born. I have a warm feeling toward those moving heroic endeavors of my brethren. With all my heart I wish them to be able to create a sunny shelter for as many oppressed people as possible. But I could never think of it as of something of my own.

I rather feel that Jewish nationalism demeans Judaism itself. The essential ideal of Judaism is the ideal of Messianism, the yearning for brotherly coexistence of humanity and of uniting all endeavors to uplift universal happiness.

The duty of every man is to pave the way for the awaited one and to contribute to the coming of these times. Such yearning is dormant in the heart of every Jew, no matter whether he is a practicing Jew or not.

The world, through its terrible cataclysms, is nevertheless aiming toward this end. I am convinced that sooner or later it will be reached. Meanwhile the world is still very young. Europe is a few thousand years younger than the Jews. She gears all her energy and passion toward things non-essential. In the past, it used to be religious differences, now it is national disparities, and tomorrow it will be a power struggle under different mottoes. Humanity squanders its energy on such non-essentials instead of uniting to fight the real enemy with the adverse power of nature, with its avarice, poverty, vast extent, sickness, and death.

History integrated Jews into many nations and they became their faithful sons. They adopted their languages as their own. They have served faithfully those nations who have let them do so. They preserve a sentiment for the countries in which they had lived for centuries but from which they were eventually expelled. They retained for over seven centuries after expulsion the old German jargon that they diffused since the Crusaders' persecutions in the Rhine countries. The Sephardic Jews speak Spanish to this day, although 500 years have elapsed since the horrors of the Holy Inquisition.

The dispersion, which was looked upon as a curse, became in a way a blessing, because, while keeping deep in their hearts the Messianic ideals of brotherly coexistence of the nations, they found themselves in a position enabling them to become the pioneers of future humanity.

Their achievements toward universal progress are enormous in many areas. In the background of my own life I saw in passing great figures such as Einstein,[366] Bergson,[367] Alfred Adler,[368] Freud,[369] great creators, physicians, great inventors, and chemists. The percentage of Jewish Nobel laureates outnumbers by far the percentage of Jews among the white race.

Palestine is a symptom of disease; a symptom of infection by the venom of the nationalism prevailing nowadays. It is forsaking directions from time immemorial and entering the road of false prophets of the moment. It is abandoning the road of greatness in service to humanity and choosing the narrow limited path of its own "folk."

I entered upon my work with enthusiasm. I had to open the road for various items of Polish production. The ground was easy and the population not only full of initiative but—despite everything—friendly toward Poland. Many areas needed help [in products] such as lumber, wooden crates, cattle, butter, textiles, and iron. During my two-year work, imports from Poland to Palestine rose from thirteenth to sixth place according to their local statistics. We took the lead over such competitors as France, Italy, Belgium, and Czechoslovakia. The work was interesting and gave me satisfaction.

Unfortunately, my superior was Consul Łukaszewicz,[370] born in the Siberian city of Chita, lacking a college education, unfamiliar with foreign languages, and completely ignorant in economics. The only qualification he possessed was that he once belonged to the Polish intelligence service and was an "inside man." He hated me from the first moment. He could not stand a subordinate who topped him in every way. This animosity increased despite my humble behavior toward him. On top of that, the Department of Foreign Affairs was dispatching my

---

366 Albert Einstein (1879–1955), a theoretical physicist, philosopher, and author who is widely regarded as one of the most influential and best known scientists and intellectuals of all time.

367 Henri-Louis Bergson (1859–1941), a major French philosopher, influential especially in the first half of the twentieth century.

368 Alfred Adler (1870–1937), an Austrian medical doctor, psychologist, and founder of the school of individual psychology.

369 Sigmund Freud (born Sigismund Schlomo Freud, 1856–1939), a Jewish Austrian neurologist who founded the psychoanalytic school of psychiatry.

370 Stanisław Łukaszewicz (1892–1951), a Polish diplomat.

reports to other consulates to serve as examples, and my office was full of clients while his remained empty.

He treated me so badly that by the end of 1936, I returned home.

My mother died during my absence. The attorney managed things better than I could have hoped for. The financial status was somehow improving.

Only the glass factory administered by the workers was a sad example of mismanagement. The workmen's cooperative was fully supported by the government. Their taxes were lowered, prices of railroad transport as well as coal were reduced, and delayed payments for social security were tolerated. During all this time I received no payment from their cooperative due to me as rent. Despite this situation, the workmen's wages were behind for weeks. The first administration elected by the workmen wound up in jail for corruption. The second one, together with the government agent, was stealing more discreetly but just as efficiently, accepting illegal commissions for merchandise sold below the normal price. The buildings, machinery, and roofs were in shambles. Some machines and molds were stolen and sold, nobody knew by whom and where. Even one unfinished building was taken apart and the bricks were sold.

I was even more concerned about the situation of my son. I could help him financially only in a very small way. After his high school graduation, I wanted him to serve his year of military service. However, he was not accepted, declared "unfit" with the "C" category. While some people tried to extricate their sons from military service, I went out of my way to try to get him in. I went to Gen. Popowicz,[371] commander of the Lwów corps, whom I knew well. I told him that Adam had that year won a championship of the City of Lwów for backstroke swimming, and also first prize for a 20-kilometer ski race with a gun. I also told him that my father was an officer, that I was one, and would like my son to become one too in the future. The general told me frankly that the percentage of Jewish high school graduates was so big

---

371 Bolesław Popowicz (1878–1937), brigadier general of the Polish Army, commander of the 6th District Corps in Lwów between March 1928 and October 1935.

that the recruiting boards were instructed to sift the applicants and make sure that the reserve officers corps be not overwhelmingly Jewish. For me, however, he would comply. Next year, I gave him Adam's application, on which he marked with red pencil "I approve." Thus, my son was accepted to the army in this unusual manner. He was the best in his class; he was among the first to advance and never met with discrimination during his military service.

At the universities, an antisemitic mood prevailed. Jewish students were beaten by colleagues, cut with razor blades, thrown down the stairs; lone students were attacked by groups and beaten with clubs; there were even cases of murder. At first the "numerus clausus" was proclaimed, then "numerus nullus." The university authorities looked away when Jewish students were forced to sit on separate benches called "University Ghetto." I did not want to send my children to such schools under these conditions. I still hoped that this situation would change one day and I wanted my children to love Poland. To achieve this, they must be spared such an experience.

Adam attended only one year of the Commercial Academy, and Ajusia went to the Ecole Supérieure de Sécretariat in Brussels. At the time I returned from Palestine, Adam was unemployed and was looking for any kind of a job, even part-time, in Warsaw.

While I was at my consular post, I did some favors for the Robinson company, very active exporters of bacon.[372] I thought that if they could employ Adam, he would learn the international trade on a large scale. Robinson himself was a Jew, but he had to decline my request; he received instructions from the Department of Industry and Trade not to hire Jews. They wanted to train "their own people" even in this area.

I felt more and more like a stranger. Often I caught myself thinking about Poles as "they," while all my previous life I never thought of them as other than "we." Still, my reaction was relatively moderate, as I was too deeply involved with all that was Polish. But I am not at all

---

372 Oskar Robinson, Bydgoszcz, 2 Piotra Skargi St., Exportation de Boeufs et de Porcs. See *Polski przemysł i handel: rynek polski: księga adresowa i informacyjna przedsiębiorstw przemysłowych, handlowych i finansowych w Rzeczypospolitej Polskiej* (Warsaw: Izba Przemysłowo-Handlowa, 1930), 663.

surprised at the extreme revolutionary reaction of the desperate Jewish youth, who did not grow up in the Polish tradition and were oppressed, rejected, and becoming poorer and poorer.

Smolka[373] was correct when he said in the Diet [of Galicia] in 1867 that one cannot oppress the minority and expect their loyalty. Following times of oppression, one must first grant the people full and true equality and then wait a few generations for the results, for the return of mental equilibrium of those who formerly suffered.

The Armenian problem never existed in Poland despite the fact that Armenians were also a different race. For centuries they enjoyed true equality; they were allowed to own land and hold public office. That's why they became citizens like all others. It is the only way to instill in Jews the Polish spirit, instead of artificially instigating the element of separation.

The ruling majority of society is always responsible for the attitude of the minority. Every nation has such Jews as they deserve.[374]

I finally succeeded in placing Adam in the "Western Bank." This bank derived from the bank of the Wawelbergs, who were in close relations with the Liliens' bank. Adam was a good worker, was moved to different departments, and advanced quickly.

I, myself, found a new field of business in promoting and patenting new inventions and establishing contracts for their production. In Poland, this was quite a new field, which gave me independence and allowed me to work from my home, without any contact with the authorities. This was most important for me, as all contacts with the authorities always turned out to be ghastly.

In this connection, I went to London in early 1937; I stayed there for several months, conducted some business, and made some useful contacts. When I returned home, I continued correspondence, and business started to develop. My first income began flowing in.

And so I lived in seclusion at Zofiówka and, rain or shine, I cut wood to heat water for my bath.

---

373 A famous governor of Galicia [J.G.]. See above, note 151.

374 "Jedes Land hat die Juden, die es verdient," a saying by Karl Emil Franzos, "Todte Seelen," *Neue Freie Presse*, 31 March 1875, 2.

The workmen's cooperative declared itself bankrupt and the glass factory had to close down. They left behind buildings in ruin, machines in disrepair, huge debts, and hungry, unpaid workers. The money due us for the rent was unpaid too.

A delegation of workers came to me. I knew well these people and liked them. Their grandfathers had worked in the factory under my grandfather, their fathers under my own father. I held their children for christening and came to their weddings. Their families lived with us for a hundred years,[375] and the factory gave them houses free of rent, as well as parcels of land to cultivate. Now, they came to ask that I personally take the lead and put the factory back to work:

"Because, Mr. Proprietor," they said, "it's always good to have a master. This way, there is someone to argue with, someone to strike against, but somehow it always turns out right."

"But you know very well that a lot of money is needed to run the factory and I don't have it any more," I replied.

"So maybe you will find someone to whom to lease the factory."

I found someone and signed a contract. He was already making the necessary repairs to set the factory in motion, when the county ordered to build a few kilometers of elegant fence. Frictions with administration began when World War II broke out.

✎ ✎ ✎

Adam was at that time on maneuvers in Stryj[376] with his regiment. Ajusia was in Brussels. My wife's cousin Lola[377] and her daughter Zosia[378] from Kraków showed up at Zofiówka. Mania[379] was at home.

I went every day to the Corps District Command, trying to be inducted into the army. There were hundreds of people in a similar position. Among others, I met General Kukiel.

---

375 The glass factory in Żółkiew was founded in 1854.
376 Presently Stryi in Lviv oblast, Ukraine.
377 Lola Wachtel née May. Lola was married to Marian Jerzy Wachtel (1894–ca. 1941) [J.G.].
378 Zofia Wachtel (b. 1921) was persecuted by the Soviets in 1942. She was married to Jerzy Wajdowicz after the war [J.G.].
379 Marya Lilien [J.G.].

"If only they gave us a gun and allowed us to take the risk."

They didn't. It happened that I was accepted as a voluntary officer-translator to a department at the headquarters of the commander-in-chief, by Major Włodzimierz Dąbrowski,[380] who took the responsibility upon himself and accepted me without any formalities. For this, I will always be indebted to him.

The Germans were already firing on us with their artillery when we filled our vehicles with gasoline. Mania left in an adventurous way. Lola went to Brody for "better shelter."[381] She wound up in Siberia! My devoted friend,[382] secretary at the railroad, and Marynia, my beloved old nurse who lived under our roof for fifty years, stayed at home. The gardener, Lachaut, with his wife and children, also remained.

Our unit rushed along the eastern borders of the country and finally, without any special adventures, landed in Romania on 19 September. With heavy hearts we crossed the border bridge over the Czeremosz River.

In Bukovina, the goodhearted Major Dąbrowski exchanged the Army Treasury Polish zlotys into dollars at the official rate. Thus, instead of 350 worthless zlotys, I came into possession of about $70, which at that time represented there quite a considerable amount.

The Romanians directed us to Vatra Dornei and placed us in decent hotels. I had this good feeling that it began well, but that it would finish behind bars. I bought civilian clothes, assembled some small luggage, and went to Bucharest. I reported again to the army and was rejected.

I started giving English lessons and volunteered to work with the Red Cross. Very soon after that, a delegation of the Quaker Society of

---

380 Probably Major Włodzimierz Dąbrowski, who headed Office "B" (responsible for the East), in 1937–1939. This office prepared clandestine actions against the Soviet Union, conducting "Promethean operations" among non-Russian peoples (e.g. Caucasus, Tatar, Ukrainian, and Cossack émigrés) and creating covert organizations along Poland's borders with Soviet Belarus and Ukraine.

381 My grandmother Ewa (my mother's mother) lived in Brody, near the Polish-Russian border [J.G.]. Ewelina Chawa Abranowicz née May.

382 Fifka [J.G.].

Friends arrived in order to help the Polish refugees. They hired me and my new job gave me full satisfaction, allowing me to live in comfort.

News from Zofiówka began arriving. The Russians requisitioned the ground floor and opened some sort of a club. They cleared out the furniture from downstairs. They only took the cabinets from the library and threw out the books into the garden. My friend[383] picked them up and stored them in the attic. Upstairs, she gave shelter to quite a number of friends and for the time being they were left in peace. They paid rent to the Bolsheviks for living in my house. They gave my garden to the gardener as a present. He loyally supplied fruit and vegetables to my friend and regularly reported all his activities to her. I received these reports in Bucharest.

Old Marynia was ordered to leave. She went to bed and died of grief. My friend, when writing me about her funeral, said: "How happy she is now!"

Later, when the Germans arrived, they completely ruined everything. None of our friends or family remained. The rest of the furniture was sent to Germany or burned. Even our old trees in the park were cut down.

In Romania I met with my younger sister Mania. She is very talented and full of imagination. She finished her studies of architecture at the Polytechnic School in Lwów and was always interested in the arts. For a few years, she studied in the United States with the famous architect Frank Lloyd Wright. She loved Zofiówka as much as I did and was always returning there. Now, after many adventures, she managed to get out of the country with a convoy of the Polish Artillery. In Bucharest, she was helped by a friend she had met in America, who was married to a Romanian general, Brătescu,[384] former aide-de-camp to Queen Maria.[385] Later, Gen. Brătescu was taken prisoner at

---

383 The above-mentioned Fifka [J.G.].
384 Constantin Brătescu (1892–1971), a Romanian major-general during World War II. Following the surrender of Friedrich Paulus's 6th Army at the Battle of Stalingrad, Brătescu became a prisoner of war and was held captive from 1943 to 1948.
385 Marie of Romania (Marie Alexandra Victoria, previously Princess Marie of Edinburgh; 1875–1938), a British princess by birth and Romanian queen by marriage.

Marya Lilien, portrait by Antoni Michalak, ca. 1938. Canvas, oil.
Courtesy of Duncan Grant

Stalingrad. After a while, Mania received an American visa and left for the USA via then still neutral Italy.

I thought that in America she would live with our sister Klara,[386] who in 1913 married Bloomfield, an American citizen and our distant cousin.[387] He is a chemical engineer and made some kind of invention. They are well off and own a beautiful home on wooded grounds on Elkhart Lake in Wisconsin. They also have a lovely daughter, Margitka.[388]

---

386 Klara Janina Bloomfield née Lilien.
387 Grover Bloomfield (1892–?).
388 Margaret Jane Grant née Bloomfield.

Klara was like Mania, always full of enthusiasm for the arts. She devoted herself to music. She played the piano under the guidance of Teodor Pollak, but later she mostly sang. She studied voice with the foremost masters, first Lombardi in Florence,[389] then Sembrich-Kochańska[390] in New York, and finally Yvette Guilbert[391] in Paris. She chose to be a diseuse[392] and with great subtlety interpreted folk songs of many nations and epochs. She gave public performances in America, Paris, Vienna, and Warsaw and had excellent reviews. Later, she limited herself to teaching and concerts for small chosen audiences. Lately, she has been working on a wonderful project—the History of the Song. She collects material, classifies it, adds comments, and gives lectures illustrated by her own singing voice.

Mania, however, did not content herself with a comfortable way of life at her sister's side. The restless blood of the Liliens, the artistic instincts, and the drive to creative independence got the best of her. Very soon [after moving to the USA] she worked out a position for herself, and to this day she lectures on the Art of Interior Design at the Art Institute of Chicago. Both my sisters are outstanding.

I sent a telegram to my daughter in Brussels, informing her of my arrival in Bucharest. In reply, I received news that Adam was alive in Hungary. After heavy battles of the 1939 campaign, he was the only officer of his battalion left alive who, together with sixty survivors, succeeded in crossing over the Carpathian Mountains into Hungary, where he was interned. Klara offered to obtain an American visa for him, to send him money and civilian clothes, but he declined, saying that he was an officer and the war was not yet over. Some time later, he succeeded in escaping from the camp and crossed over into Yugoslavia.

---

389 Vincenzo Lombardi was also a teacher of Enrico Caruso.
390 Marcella Sembrich (1858–1935) was the stage name of the Polish coloratura soprano Prakseda Marcelina Kochańska. She had an important international singing career, chiefly at the New York Metropolitan Opera and the Royal Opera House, Covent Garden, London.
391 Yvette Guilbert (1865–1944), a French cabaret singer and actress of the Belle Époque.
392 Diseuse is an actress who presents dramatic recitals, sometimes accompanied by a male music counterpart.

From there he went via Greece to Syria, where Colonel Kopański[393] was just organizing his famous Carpathian Brigade. At this time, he is still serving on the staff of this unit and has participated in all its exploits.

After the capitulation of France, General Mittelhausser[394] wanted to disarm the Carpathian Brigade. In response, Colonel Kopański firmly declared that in such a case it would be the first time in history that the Polish Army would have to shoot at French soldiers. Mittlehauser relented, allowing the Polish Army to proceed to Palestine. However, he was adamant that they leave the cannons behind, but Kopański had already arranged that the cannons be sent ahead of the army. Mittlehauser gave the order to have them returned and threatened to have Kopański interned until the cannons were back.

Adam was sent to Palestine together with Capt. Kaliński[395] in order "to claim the cannons." They informed the British authorities that the Brigade was arriving with the intention to submit itself to the British command in Palestine. They explained to the British authorities the problem about the cannons and stressed the dangerous situation of their commander. As a result, the British authorities advised Mittelhauser that the British Army would march into Syria if Kopański was not immediately released. This was how the Carpathian Brigade, together with their arms and their leader, wound up under British command in Palestine.

While on the staff of the Carpathian Brigade, Adam participated in the entire Libyan campaign, the siege of Tobruk and Gazala. Later, when he returned to Palestine and Iraq, after the influx of Polish soldiers from Russia, the brigade was transformed into a division. While on the staff of the Carpathian Division, he from the beginning continuously participated in the Italian campaign, performing well in

---

393 Stanisław Kopański (1895–1976), a Polish military commander. One of the best-educated Polish officers of the time, he served with distinction in World War II. He is best known as the creator and commander of the Polish Independent Carpathian Brigade and the Polish 3rd Carpathian Infantry Division. In 1943–1946, he was chief of staff of the commander-in-chief of the Polish Armed Forces in the West.
394 Eugène-Désiré-Antoine Mittelhausser (1873–1949), a French general.
395 Jan Marian Kaliński (1902–1944), a Polish infantry officer.

the battles of Monte Cassino and Ancona. General Kopański spoke to me in a very superlative way about him. He received several distinctions and was promoted.

My own adventures were less dramatic. The German pressure on Romania was becoming greater and the situation of Polish refugees more precarious.

In the fall of 1940, the Society of Friends[396] persuaded the British government to take interest in the fate of the Poles in Romania, who were threatened by the imminent German invasion. His Majesty's Government invited a group of 500 people to Cyprus and I found myself in this group.

We spent the first night after landing in quarantine. There was place only for women and children in the barracks, and men had to sleep on mattresses outdoors under the naked sky. I lay down and looked at the passing shadows. I heard whispers: "Mr. Governor," "Mr. General," "Mr. Minister"—and suddenly I realized that it was yesterday's Poland wasting away here on naked soil. And this was only the luckiest group that managed to escape the German concentration camps and the camps in Soviet Russia. They unfolded before me like the ghosts of the dead past.

I saw ghosts twice before. The first time was when some drunken Russian aristocrats came to visit my friend Gonczarow at Zofiówka. They continued to drink to my health:

"Here is a man. One should walk three kilometers to come across a man. Do you know, Doctor, whom have I brought to you? This is Graf Lelawski, a secular General-in-Chief of His Emperor's Majesty, Marshal of Nobility of the Podolian Governorate, Parliament Member."

"Well, Doctor, all this has been and has passed. Now only a specter remains."

They continued to drink. One of them was crying, another mumbled in Russian:

"Doctor, tell me that I am dumb. I am not dumb, I am a gentleman …"

The second time I saw ghosts was in 1937. After many years of absence, I found myself again in Vienna and I dropped in at the Hunters

---

396 Quakers [J.G.].

Club. On the surface it seemed as if nothing had changed. They had only aged and faded somewhat. The same doorman opened the door. The same attendant took my coat. The same portrait of Archduke Franz Ferdinand in hunter's attire looked from the wall. The same "His Excellency," "Herr Graf," "Herr Hofrat," and "Herr Baron" sat at the bridge table and with trembling hands played for pennies, while outside the world had turned over. Sometimes on such occasions I had the feeling that I too was only a ghost, that I wasn't even a man of yesterday. I had no influence. I felt that I was a man of the past, lost among the present times. That Don Quixote was my only brother.

I realized then that the foundations of my feelings and thoughts, the ones based on the teachings of the Jewish prophets, the yearning for a universal brotherhood, the sense of duty to bring this brotherhood closer—all this belongs to the future, to the distant tomorrow. And as a naked man thrown into the waves of the lonely fight for existence, I actually felt better armed and stronger than those ghosts.

My thoughts continued to wander. I began to realize that it did not concern me alone. I think this explains how Jews could survive thousands of years under such dire conditions. It is the Messianic idea, the thoughts of Isaiah and Jeremiah, that give us our eternal youth.

⟋ ⟋ ⟋

The next day on Cyprus, we were placed in excellent hotels, surrounded by comfort, and treated with respect. The governor himself came first to visit us.

Among us there were about 100 Polish officers, headed by Col. Epler.[397] He was from Lwów, an old veteran, who in 1939 improvised the Kobryń Division, fought the Germans and the Bolsheviks with them, and was the last to surrender. This happened after five weeks of fighting, when the ammunition was completely used up during his victorious battle at Kock. I became something like his aide-de-camp and translated his excellent war memoirs into English. We were invited

---

397 Adam Józef Epler (1891–1965). See his book, *Ostatni żołnierz polski kampanii roku 1939* (London: Wydział Prac Kult.-Ośw. Ministerstwa Obrony Narodowej, 1943).

together by the local dignitaries and to military camps and we gave lectures to the British officers' corps.

In June 1941, when the Germans occupied the isle of Crete, we were sent to Palestine in order to be in a safer place. Again, I tried to join the army and was refused. In vain, I wrote on this matter to several generals and reported to them personally. One day, when I was due to go to Rhodesia, I received a letter from Gen. Kopański from Tobruk. He had telegraphed headquarters in London, requesting that I be recruited as an officer translator for the Polish army. Again, I waited in vain.

It was a great joy to meet with my son. How many things had happened since I last saw him! How many times did my heart go out to him while I anxiously waited for news about him! As far as my daughter was concerned, I only knew that she had managed to escape to the unoccupied part of France and that she was trying to go to America, but the Spaniards posed difficulties in transit. I thought of her with great concern and often remembered the rhymes torn out of my heart:

Cóż za ojciec, co dzieciom ojcem być nie może?
Och, bądźże Ty im Ojcem, Wiekuisty Boże![398]

Somehow I settled down and somehow I lived. It was strange how easy it was to be a refugee. When I was crossing over the border bridge on the Czeremosz River, I was sure I was starting a terrible life of a humiliated wanderer. Instead, after a year of comfortable existence in Bucharest, after nine months of life in luxury in a Cyprus hotel, I found myself in Palestine, in the midst of well-organized social welfare. There was a delegate of the [British] government and there was a committee for the refugees. There was medical care, a club house, good and inexpensive food; there were lectures and a school for children, and we

---

398 "What father is it who cannot be a father to his children?/ You be their father, Oh Eternal God!" These lines are from the poem "Rozmowy z Janem" (Dialogues with Jan), written by Józef Andrzej Teslar (1889–1961) in September–November 1942, dedicated to Jan Śliwiński, and published in *Wiadomości Polskie* [London], 30 January 1944, p. 1. Teslar was a Polish officer, physician, poet, journalist, translator, and a lecturer in Polish language and culture at the University of Glasgow in 1942–1945.

were regularly receiving modest subsidies that allowed for quite a decent living. When I thought of my people who remained in the country or were deported by the occupants, I could not understand why and by what right was I so privileged.

And thus another year went by. I wrote articles, gave lectures. I spent time with acquaintances in Café Yamiah on the sea. The café was nicknamed "The Parliament" because Poles assembled there every day for an hour of "saving their country." I became interested in the English political press and began to disseminate among the refugees the results of my studies of many facets of this literature. It included such subjects as organization and mutual relationship of nations after the war, socio-economic reforms, guarantee of human rights, and postwar treatment of Germany. I also spoke on independent themes such as "What is Freedom."

Once I was invited to give a lecture in German to the local Jewish intellectual elite. At that time, I also read some psycho-analytical works by Alfred Adler. I was quite impressed by the contrast between the two primary motifs of human behavior, "Gemeinschaftssinn" and "Geltungsdrang."[399] This is the key to understanding not only the way of life and conduct of people, but also the political and collective phenomena. It shows in a new scientific light the old differentiation between evil and good, haughtiness and love, *superbia* and *caritas*.[400]

Sometimes I smiled with pity at myself and my "education." I realized that not only any engineer or physician, but also every shoemaker, carpenter, watchmaker, or bookbinder is better equipped to earn a living among strangers than myself. It turned out, however, that my knowledge of many languages came in useful as a weapon.

In July 1942, I was engaged by the British Military Mission as a teacher of English to the men in the Polish divisions. I wound up in the Carpathian Division, where I met with my son. Despite the fact that I was receiving my wages from the British, Gen. Kopański allowed me to wear my Polish officer's uniform. I was assigned to the headquarters of

---

399 "Sense of community" and "desire for recognition" [J.G.].
400 Contempt and charity [J.G.].

the 2nd Brigade and finally could start living in a camp atmosphere among colleagues.

I felt at home among them. In Syria, I often served as a liaison officer assigned to high level personalities, both English and French. Once we attended a big reception in the desert under the stately tents of the Bedouin Emir Fuad, brother-in-law of Ibn Saud.[401]

Later, I made a long journey that lasted an entire month. It took me from Damascus via Haifa, Suez, Aden, Basra, and Baghdad to Mosul. There I had many students and even Gen. Kopański attended my lessons together with his chief of staff. I was charmed by Kopański's personality, as was everyone who met him. He is a man conscious of his own value, therefore he can afford to be modest. Not only does he not let people feel his superiority, but he tries to strengthen their own importance and self-esteem.

In the mountains of northern Iraq, I had the opportunity to come across the Kurds and also a strange sect of Yazidi,[402] worshipers of Satan. I made some interesting notes about their beliefs and customs. I also met the renowned archeologist Seton Lloyd,[403] who personally showed me Nineveh and his latest excavations revealing an unknown ancient civilization dating from before the Assyrians.

Here I learned about the miraculous escape of my daughter.

When Hitler invaded Marseilles, I was desperate and prepared for the worst. I climbed high on the hills and, facing in the direction of southern France, strained to send her my ardent blessings via some imaginary radioactivity. Suddenly, I received a puzzling telegram from Lisbon. Then, a letter from her in French: "Mon cher oncle Arthur, je

---

401 Ibn Saud (Abdulaziz, 1876–1953), the first monarch of Saudi Arabia, the third Saudi state.

402 The Yazidi (also Yezidi) are members of a Kurdish religion with ancient Indo-European roots. Speculations around the erroneous opinion that the Yazidis worship Satan have continued since the nineteenth century. Cf. Alexander Pushkin, "Notice sur la Secte des Yézidis" (1835).

403 Seton Howard Frederick Lloyd (1902–1996), an English archaeologist. He was president of the British School of Archaeology in Iraq, director of the British Institute of Archaeology at Ankara (president, 1948–1961), and professor of Western Asiatic archaeology at the Institute of Archaeology, University of London (1962–1969).

Joanna Lilien, 1938, Lwów. Courtesy of Catherine Grun

suis en train d'aller en Angleterre . . . Que j'aimerais te revoir bientôt dans notre cher Canada,"[404] and an unknown signature. It was explained to me that she was probably given a role to play. After a while, a telegram came from England: "My husband is in a Spanish concentration camp. Help us to get him out." I was bewildered. I was in Mosul; he was in Miranda de Ebro. How did this child imagine that a father could do anything. But after a while—why not try? I became incited to action.

---

404 "My dear Uncle Arthur, I am on my way to England . . . How I would love to see you soon in our beloved Canada!" [J.G.].

Upon my request, the British consul sent a wire to his colleague in Bilbao. Something had moved. It came to light that on the other end, another British consul had procured a Canadian passport for your mother and she was saved this way. Now they helped your father too.

And this is how you could come into this world, my darling.

When the army was scheduled to leave Iraq, I returned to Palestine and again tried unsuccessfully to be accepted into the Polish army. I then applied for acceptance into the British army. In the meantime I gave lessons. Since the rent for apartments was high, I rented a flat roof of a small house. I opened an army cot, spread Persian carpets, and with good humor I climbed a ladder to my "apartment." Later, I was again invited to one of the Polish camps. General Sosnkowski arrived in Palestine; I wrote him to remind him of our earlier encounters. I mentioned that the British are willing to take me to their army. Couldn't I, however, be of use in our own troops? He responded that my advanced age . . . etc, etc.

I was hurt in a car accident. The British sent me to an excellent military health resort, where I was cured. I recovered and received an order to immediately report to the General Staff in Cairo. I started service on 5 January 1944.

I am a press censor and perform a very interesting and responsible job. From the first moment I experienced here a cordial comradeship and complete trust in my person. I started as a second lieutenant, but after fourteen days I was promoted to lieutenant, and after two months I became a captain. I am surrounded by pleasant, educated, and decent people. There is only friendship here—no envy, no intrigues or jealousy—only true comradeship. It has been a long time since I lived in such a pleasant atmosphere. If I ever happen to dream of a guardian angel, strangely, he always has an English face. He has taken me under his protective wings since my Romanian times. He drove me out to Cyprus, looked after me in Palestine, gave me work, and then a prestigious position as an officer. He has fed me, dressed me while in exile, and led me into the midst of lively, pulsating existence. He gave me the best environment and friends. And above all, he saved my dearest daughter. It is impossible to repay such a debt of gratitude. I, however, still expect from him something more, because now all hopes for a better world are linked to him.

Our civilization has developed to such a degree that it must be organized to comprise the total globe, or else it must perish. The technical advances are such that with proper organization, humanity can live in happiness and wealth, with all the necessities well provided for. Without organization, all progress and every invention will deprive others of work and, instead of being a blessing, will become a curse. Because of the advancement of the technology of destruction, there will be no peace or safety as long as at least one point on the globe enjoys a total "sovereignty" and can prepare for new aggressions backed by secret arsenals and scientific laboratories.

The world must have a centralized organization and leadership. The vision of a peace backed by several centers of political power and united only by an understanding or an alliance is utopian and will undoubtedly lead to the next, still more ghastly, war. It will disappoint those who think that world organization can rely only on goodwill and understanding. It will be impossible not to apply force.

The best solution would be if the angels could take over this difficult task. Unfortunately, they are not at our disposal. Among men, till recently, there have been four candidates: Russia, Germany, Anglo-Saxons, and Japan. In this ballot, I would cast my vote for the Anglo-Saxons. Although they, too, are only humans, with human imperfections, of these four nations they possess most of the moral values; they have the most sense of responsibility as rulers toward their subordinates in the sense of "live and let live." They also have the least ambition for power, and therefore are most qualified to be the leaders.

And this is what I expect of them, and the world expects too.

The world in its terrible struggle found itself confronting a dreadful dilemma. It fights its enemy, Satan, but calls upon Beelzebub[405] for help as an ally. After the victory, the world will have to get rid of this ally, but Beelzebub possesses all the diabolical shrewdness and is aware that after the victory he will have to deal with resistance. As long as Satan

---

405 Meaning Russia. This entire paragraph is about Russia [M.L.].

is not defeated, he will face no resolute opposition. He wants to master the world. Therefore now, before the final victory, he quickly creates *faits accomplis* and gains strategic positions for a future final battle. He grows, inflating beyond any measure, and speaks as an arbiter of virtue.

The danger is serious. The Anglo-Saxon masses, who like to feel comfortable in their reasoning, see the world not as it actually is but as they would like it to be. Disputes arise between England and the USA, where unity should prevail. For the second time during this war, the French betray the civilization to which they belong. The Czechs became "the Devil's advocates" helping Beelzebub to penetrate into the heart of Europe. The Americans were maneuvered into a situation in which they might stand before a fatal dilemma—isolationism or imperialism.

In this tragic moment, in my mind the picture of Poland went through a second metamorphosis. She again became great and pathetic. Crammed between colossal cannibals, torn apart, oppressed, soaked in the blood of millions, betrayed and assailed by a storm of slander and ridicule; somehow, in her tragedy, she rose to some incredible moral heights. In the face of the magnitude of suffering, the memories of the uncontrolled mobs, of Brześć and Bereza,[406] and the pogroms, the painted fences[407] now seemed insignificant. Instead, a hero emerged with an innocent child's face, a knight without blemish, and old visions of our romantic poetry came to mind. Was it Christ among nations [as described] by Adam Mickiewicz?[408] No, this might be too far-fetched. But it was Słowacki's "Winkelried of Nations."[409]

I can visualize this Swiss peasant rushing to Sempach, dressed in leather clothes, among his comrades armed only with axes and sticks

---

406 Cruel detention camps for political rebels in Poland [M.L.].
407 Probably referring to marked fences to target the victims of hatred.
408 Adam Mickiewicz evoked the vision of Poland as the "Christ of nations" in his drama *Dziady* (part III, written in 1832).
409 Arnold von Winkelried is a legendary hero of Swiss history. Winkelried's sacrifice brought about the victory of the Old Swiss Confederacy in the Battle of Sempach (1386) against the army of the Habsburg Duke Leopold III of Austria. Polish Romantic poet Juliusz Słowacki (1809–1849) used the representation of Winkelried in his dramatic poem "Kordian" (1833), where the protagonist decides to kill the Tsar of Russia to take Poland's suffering on himself, easing a breakthrough to freedom for his nation. Słowacki considered Poland the "Winkelried of Nations."

against the wall of steel of the Habsburg warriors. I can see how in the rage of the battle he grabs the enemy lances, drives them into his own chest, shouting: "Forward brothers, I will clear your way!"

Nobody questions what kind of a man Winkelried was in his daily life. Maybe he was a drunkard, maybe he even hurt his own children. However, the glory of his act, the magnitude of his sacrifice redeeming the victory, has been remembered for centuries. My own country played this heroic, tragic, role in 1939 and must now play it again for a second time.

At first, while Europe was asleep, my country roused her with her powerful protest "NO." She roused her at the last moment when rescue was still possible. She fought alone the horrible battle of cavalry against tanks and airplanes, and, finally, betrayed and stabbed in the back, was defeated and crumbled in ruins.[410]

But in spite of her defeat she did not stop fighting. Whoever was able took up arms. The elderly pretended to be young, children pretended to be grown up; anything just to be inducted into the armed forces, to be able to continue the fight. And they fought like lions. They were thrown into the most dangerous spots. They fought at Narwik, Tobruk, Monte Cassino, Falaise, Arnhem, and Breda. They flew over London when German bombers were using Russian fuel and Molotov[411] was banqueting with Ribbentrop.[412] The handful of Polish pilots accounted for only ten percent of all planes flying at that time over England, but they shot down twenty percent of all German planes destroyed during the Battle of Britain. The first shot fired against the cruiser *Bismarck* came from a Polish vessel.

And now, tortured and almost bled to death, she again cries "NO" to the scheming of the other monster who wants to swallow the world over her dead body. Again, the world is asleep, half hypnotized. It has to be awakened through a new sacrifice by Poland. The impoverished people of Warsaw stand up and scream to the four corners of the world

---

410 The author refers to World War II, when the Germans attacked Poland and the Russians hit her from the rear [M.L.].
411 Vyacheslav Mikhailovich Molotov (1890–1986), the Soviet foreign minister.
412 Joachim von Ribbentrop (1893–1946), the foreign minister of Nazi Germany.

that they want neither Germans nor Russians. By the holocaust of Warsaw, they apply the seal to this historic document.[413]

And thus they fight heroically in defense of our great civilization while their own homes are in ruins and the fight sometimes seems hopeless. They stand again at the ancient frontiers and, as did their fathers, they form with their own bodies a bulwark of Christianity.

How insignificant are now the memories of all empty slogans like "strong, together, ready," how worthless are the inevitable ugly quarrels among the emigrants. I shudder when I think of the new meaning that present times give to the words of Wyspiański: "Poland is a great thing."[414]

It seems sometimes that the sacrifice is in vain. Sometimes one loses heart, and it seems that the waves of Pankracy's red hordes will overrun crumbling Okopy.[415] The whole civilized world seems to be like the hotel lobby in Sholem Asch's novel. People are sitting around helplessly inside the building while in the streets the rabble is raging. Slowly, strange figures emerge from basements and sit down with mocking smiles, certain that soon their underground world of false security will also be flooded.[416] The last traces of chivalry disappear, the old criteria of good and evil die out. And one recalls the words of Bocheński, who faced death in Poland, France, Narwik, Tobruk, Monte Cassino, and finally met it in the battle of Ancona:[417]

"It would not be proper to return from this war."

---

413 Warsaw was methodically destroyed by the Germans [M.L.].

414 Stanisław Wyspiański, *Wesele: Dramat w 3 aktach* (Kraków: Stanisław Wyspiański, 1901), act 2, scene 10.

415 The author is referring to the Romantic drama by Zygmunt Krasiński, *Nie-Boska komedia* (The Infernal Comedy), written in 1833, and exposing a struggle between the old and new orders.

416 A reference to Sholem Asch, *Three Cities*, vol. 3: *Moscow* (London: Victor Gollancz, 1933), particularly to chapter XIII: "The Servants," 667–669.

417 Adolf Maria Bocheński (1909–1944), a Polish writer and political publicist. Together with Jerzy Giedroyc, Bocheński edited the periodicals *Bunt Młodych* and *Polityka*. He authored a number of books, among them *Między Niemcami a Rosją* (Warsaw: Polityka, 1937).

Our world is holding its breath awaiting salvation by England, closely allied with America.

I firmly believe that they are not blind. Churchill[418] is not a Chamberlain;[419] Anglo-Saxons do not want to die. If they are to survive, they must remain strongly united and together they must save our world of western civilization. They must go all the way, first conquer Satan and then free themselves from Beelzebub in order to build a new world of freedom and brotherhood upon the old principles of morality.

Here and there, through momentary delusions, we perceive some good signs. The king [of England] and the president [of the United States] expressed some truth in their recent speeches.

"Defeating Germany is only half of the difficult task which we are given to perform. The second half is to build a world free of any kind of tyranny, a world worth to be lived in."[420]

When I hear these words, I am full of hope and I remember the following words by Longfellow:

Sail on, O Ship of State,
Sail on, O Union strong and great.
Humanity in all her fears,
And all her hopes for future years,
Is hanging breathless on thy fate.[421]

In Poland, too, a few shining, decent people arose at this time, such as Arciszewski[422] and Kopański, whose aim is not personal ambition but a fervent wish to serve the cause.

❦ ❦ ❦

---

418 Winston Leonard Spencer Churchill (1874–1965), a British politician, prime minister of the United Kingdom in 1940–1945, a steadfast organizer of resistance to Nazi Germany.

419 Arthur Neville Chamberlain (1869–1940), a British politician, prime minister of the United Kingdom in 1937–1940.

420 This passage loosely quotes statements by King Charles VI and President Franklin D. Roosevelt on D-Day, 6 June 1944.

421 Henry Wadsworth Longfellow, "O Ship of State" (1850).

422 Tomasz Arciszewski (1877–1955), a Polish socialist politician, prime minister of the Polish government-in-exile in London in 1944–1947.

Catherine Grun, 1945, London. *Courtesy of Catherine Grun*

My dearest Kasieńka,

I wrote all this, thinking that you and the immediate family will read it. You will find here many descriptions and a few of my own feelings and thoughts.

I fear that if others read it, many would find some passages unpleasing.

Some Poles would be offended by my frank description of the conditions prevailing in the country at that time; many a Jew will be indignant at my attitude toward Palestine; some nationalists will be offended by my non-nationalistic attitude. A progressive will dislike my approach to the revolution, a Catholic—my remarks about the Jesuits.

119

There will be many, however, who will understand me. Mostly those from among many nations for whom the continuation of our common civilization is essential. I will be understood by those whose roots are in the past and whose dream wanders toward a better future for all. There still exist such people whose thoughts are similar to mine. And if I sat among them, we could sense together, without reservations, this great word "WE."

These people will understand my deep love for my country and see that my spiritual attachment to her does not contradict, but rather supports, longing for a general organization of the world for all nations. Just as the state curbs individual anarchy, lynching, and the law of the sword, this organization must suppress anarchy and the law of the sword in the community of nations. This will bring a blessing to everybody.

This commonwealth, however, must leave to each nation its freedom of individual development, just as a state must grant a sphere of rights and freedom to each citizen. Until now, history was one of the struggle between the state and the individual for an appropriate balance between rights and duties, about how far authority can extend, and where the sphere of individual freedom begins. There will be a time when a similar struggle will embrace the question of rights and duties of nations towards their community.

They will understand that one can criticize Zionism and at the same time be deeply moved not only by the eternal Gehenna, but also by the magnitude of the Jewish mission.

They will understand the misfortunes caused by the politics of the Church in the past. At the same time, great hopes for the future will be based on it, the only survivor of the flood, the mainstay of European tradition upheld, despite everything, by the ideal of universal love.

They will also understand my view that one can loathe revolution, violence, destruction, slaughter, and rule of the populace and still be deeply aware of the necessity of progress, social reforms, planning, and the creation of conditions in which broad masses will find the kind of life worthy of a man. This because they share with me the urgent desire that all be satisfied, happy, and joyful. Maybe they will understand that one can be an enemy of Soviet Russia not because it promotes the theory of progress, but because it implements barbarian practices.

And surely many will join me in the belief that the road to progress must not lead through devastation, but should be paved by an elite controlled by the people who take their duties to heart, not intent on their own advancement; an elite who wholeheartedly adhere to the principle "noblesse oblige." As far as I am concerned, with great astonishment, since the onset of this war, I enjoy an inconceivable, undeserved, grace of God. Maybe the brilliant sunlight which always shone in my heart has somewhat faded now, but I still look at the world with hope, and my foremost wish is to give and give to others whatever is best in me.

I sense loyalty toward the wide circles to which I belong: my family, my hometown, my native region, my country, and toward the all-embracing western civilization led today by the Anglo-Saxons.

It is my fervent wish that LOVE reigns over the world, that they will beat their swords into plowshares and the wolf will dwell with the lamb. I feel that the world is ripe for some universal multinational organization and that of all the nations only the Anglo-Saxons can and should lead it in this direction.

I don't know whether I will ever see again my beloved land and my old family home. I don't know if I will ever hear the murmur of our brook; if I will ever sit on our veranda among blooming lilacs and jasmine; if I will smell the linden tree in bloom next to our home and the busy wrens will fly over my head bringing worms to their young ones. But I march forward steady and serene "Quo Deus esse iussit."[423] "Be receptive to joy as a sponge and shed sorrows like a rain cape." This is the only way to preserve one's inner strength and to give what is best in you.

∾ ∾ ∾

A Greek legend relates that when Pandora's box was opened and all the dreadful misfortunes spilled over the world, at the very end a small colorful butterfly flew out and did not stop hovering over our heads. Its name was HOPE.

A man from Nazareth, a great sufferer and saint, transformed it into a triple torch: FAITH, LOVE, HOPE.

---

423 What God commands you to be.

Thoughts of a Polish Jew

Artur Lilien-Brzozdowiecki[1]

The individual fate of a human being is not very important today. Let me, however, speak about myself, since what I have to say can illustrate a problem which nowadays is profoundly stirring so many minds and so many countries. While speaking about myself, I wish to speak about one of many; while speaking about my family, I want to speak about any family.

Lately, everywhere I hear that I am a guest in this land, that I am a foreign intruder. Seldom do I hear such claims from those who bear an old Polish cultural tradition. They are more strongly aired among those who are trying to reach, or have recently reached, the ranks of those to be reckoned with. They are voiced most brusquely among those whose grandparents or great-grandparents came to Poland as German colonists or clerks sent down here to Germanize the country. The younger generation, however, is voicing them almost in unison.

Initially, all these claims seemed to me so weird, so senseless, that I barely paid attention to them. However, when these shouts became incredibly consistent, when they were trying to drive me out of the framework of life and daily placing impediments before my son's survival, I began reflecting and asked myself whether I was in trouble,

---

1   Translation by Joanna Grun and Sergey R. Kravtsov of Artur Lilien-Brzozdowiecki "Myśli polskiego Żyda," *Polityka* 18 (163) (10 August 1938): 6, 8.

whether—at least from the standpoint of the presently dominant nationalism—there was some reason in these claims.

∽ ∽ ∽

I went again to the old Jewish cemetery, where the headstones of my progenitors, which incline toward the ground, go back to the times of the Jagiellons in an unbroken row. My thoughts ran back, tracing the living family tradition.

Here rests the Golden Rose, by whose efforts a forty-year-long litigation was settled between the Jewish community and Jesuits in Lwów. At their own expense, the Jews built a Jesuit monastery, in place of which on Hetmańska Street the Office of Internal Revenue is located today.[2] The Jesuits, in their turn, allowed the Jews to attend a small synagogue on Blacharska Street, which had been built earlier by my family.

Further along rests Nachman, son of Izak,[3] the collector of the Jewish poll tax in the days of John Casimir. When the king was in Lwów during the Cossack wars, the treasurer summoned Nachman and demanded money for military needs. Since the current taxes had already been collected, this was a matter of an advance for the next years. Nachman initiated an undertaking among the Jews. The Jews of Lwów brought money and objects of precious gold and silver until a substantial state loan reached the extent that it enabled financing the expedition. And Nachman received from the king a privilege to own a house with a six-windows-wide façade in the central square. As this was actually an exclusive prerogative of the gentry, it was an extraordinary honor for a Jew.

During their lives, the recurrent anti-Jewish riots were reminiscent of what is happening today. The perpetrators were students from urban families, the so-called *żaki*,[4] followed by the street mob. Jews called such brawls *Schülergeläuf*, i.e., students' crowds. There always appeared,

---

2   See "To Kasieńka from Grandpa," note 16.
3   Artur Lilien refers to Izak son of Nachman, and not Nachman son of Izak, as the hero of this episode in his reminiscences; cf. "To Kasieńka from Grandpa," p. 6.
4   *Żak* (from popular Lat. diacus)—a student of a Catholic school.

however, a gentleman, a governor, or a castellan, a certain Mniszech or Stadnicki, who energetically restored order.

Pensive, I went from there to the new cemetery. I stood at the grave of my grandfather Nirenstein.[5] Leon Sapieha writes in his reminiscences that once, when he had insulted the notorious governor Stadion,[6] with strong emphasis on his own Polish viewpoint, "besides [Prince] Lubomirski and Nirenstein, a banker in Lwów, nobody of the delegation dared visit me; even while meeting me in the street, they crossed to the other side in order not to greet me and thus not to compromise themselves."[7]

Not far from him rests my grandfather Artur Mises. He also enjoyed Leon Sapieha's great confidence. They jointly initiated construction of the Lwów-Kraków railway, on whose board of directors my grandfather served until his death. My grandfather cooperated with Sapieha in organizing Towarzystwo Kredytowe Ziemskie (The Landowners' Credit Union) and Galicyjska Kasa Oszczędności (The Galician Savings Bank).

Farther along rests my grandmother's brother, Herman Mises, a member of the parliament[8] in the 1870s who broached the idea of a world Polish-Jewish treaty.

Yet farther rests my grandmother, Klara Nirenstein née Mises. She was plucking lint for the insurgents in 1863[9] and published her translation of Macaulay's "About Jews."[10]

Finally, I reached my parents' grave. I remember them as people who, while working for the country and society, had almost no private life. My father, together with a group of colleagues (Romanowicz and Rutowski, among others), founded a society devoted to propagation of

---

5 The family name Nierenstein is Polonized in this article.

6 Franz Stadion, Graf von Warthausen (1806–1853), governor of Galicia in 1847–1848, Austrian minister of interior affairs and minister of education in 184–1849.

7 Leon Sapieha, *Wspomnienia* (Kraków: G. Gebethner i Spółka, 1912), 241 [note by Artur Lilien].

8 In Vienna.

9 Lint was commonly used for bandages for the wounded in those times.

10 Translation by K...a M. (Lwów, 1863) [note by Artur Lilien]. Thomas B. Macaulay, *O Żydach*, trans. K...y M. (Lwów: E. Winiarz, 1863).

the Polish polity among Jews, named "Przymierze Braci" (Covenant of Brothers).[11] They published a newspaper, *Ojczyzna* (Fatherland), and taught the Polish language, history, and literature to those children of the ghetto who turned to them. One of them was Wilhelm Feldman, later a meritorious literary critic, whom my father taught to speak Polish as a young man. My father was one of the founders and a vice-president of Czytelnia Akademicka (Academic Reading Club), now a stronghold of antisemitism, of course protected by the "Aryan paragraph."[12] Later, as a banker, he financed loans of the Lwów munic-ipality and built the Brzeżany-Podhajce railroad. Upon his initiative, Francówka,[13] a new housing area on empty meadows, was constructed and the first four-story house was built in the city. As a member of the Chamber of Commerce, he was one of those initiating construction of its imposing edifice on Akademicka Street, where his name is engraved, among others, on a memorial plaque. He also headed many social insti-tutions, sponsored vacation camps for poor children, and constantly refused to accept Austrian orders and honors. He was also on the board of the Sokół (Falcon) [sport club]. As a four-year-old child I received a Sokół uniform and still have a photo in which I pose in that costume by the feet of my comrade-father.

That same spirit animated my mother, who devoted all her thoughts and deeds to social and humanitarian work. Mother's relatives were people of such stature as Julian Klaczko and Szymon Askenazy, whose merits in the field of Polish literature are common knowledge.

It seems to me, however, that it is not true that they all came to something ready, that they only made use of things prepared by others. Rather, they were co-creators of what is surrounding us today, and traces

---

11 This society is also known as "Agudas Achim" (Heb. Agudat Aḥim, meaning, the Society of Brothers).

12 "Aryan paragraph" (German: Arierparagraph), a legal clause adopted in Nazi Germany in 1933 prohibiting Jews from filling positions in public service; in Poland—barring Jews from participation in organizations dominated by the National Democracy movement.

13 The traditional neighborhood name Franzówka is Polonized by Artur Lilien-Brzozdowiecki.

of their activity—buildings, railways, institutions, and books—are part of a still vibrant reality and are reminders of the efforts of their civic labor.

✺ ✺ ✺

I was born into that milieu, in a suburban house built by grandfather in Zofiówka near Lwów, where I still live today. As a young boy, hundreds of times I climbed every tree in the garden. Every stone, every turn of the brook, every fold of the terrain is so fused with me that perhaps they are a part of my being. The city is now expanding in our direction, but the veteran residents of the suburb, semi-peasants, look down at the newcomers, and when they speak with me use the expression: "we the locals."

I received my primary education in the private school run by the ladies Czarnowska and Dalecka, two daughters of [anti-Russian] insurgents, immigrants from Lithuania. The spirit of romantic patriotism reigned in the school. From my early childhood, I was surrounded predominantly by children from very Polish Catholic homes: the Dybowskis, Szczepanowskis, and Ramułts. Nevertheless, neither my mind nor theirs have ever been crossed by the thought that I did not fully belong to or was not equal to them. Without any shade of thought about something that separated us, I always felt myself among them as among the closest friends. Our community was based not only on amity and games, but most evidently on the same ideals that simultaneously congealed in us.

In my high school years I belonged to Promień (A Ray), a secret organization striving for independence. I took an active part in the contemporary movement of the Lwów youth, meeting at our gatherings with such people as the Skwarczyńskis, Stachiewiczs, Pasławski,[14] and Goetel. That was why I was expelled from the high school at the age of fourteen. This did not, however, disrupt my participation in the organization. The leader of our closest circle was the future general, Marian

---

14 Stefan Wiktor Pasławski (1885–1956), a general of the Polish Army.

Kukiel. I will never forget how he gathered us one November night at the graves of the [anti-Austrian] insurgents and spoke to us at length in the midst of a snowstorm. We were captivated by his speech and enthusiastically extended our arms, reciting the oath, "We swear, we swear that we will not rest and will give the last drop of our blood, until we behold Her Free and Independent!"

In those days, my father's friend from the Kingdom [of Poland],[15] Witold Jodko-Narkiewicz, one of the leaders of the underground efforts to achieve independence, frequently visited us and lived unreported in our house. Hearing his stories about schoolboys participating in the revolutionary struggle, I sold the stamp collection, which was my most precious treasure. I received a quite considerable amount of money for it, with which I bought 36 Browning pistols and handed them over to Jodko.

There, in Promień, I met Józef Piłsudski.

When later, in 1912, he met me once in the street, he stopped me and said:

"Listen to me, Lilien, you are some kind of an Austrian artillery officer. Maybe you could teach some artillery to my soldiers."

That is how I became the first artillery instructor in those primordia of the Polish Army. This episode is more fully described in "Materiały do historii artylerii legionowej" [Materials on the History of the Polish Legions' Artillery], published in *Przegląd Artyleryjski* (The Artillery Review) (February–March, 1933).[16] The trainees of that course today occupy high, even the highest, ranks in the state.

And then came the war. Despite all my efforts, I could not join the [Polish] Legions, since Austria did not discharge its artillery officers. When the Empire fell apart, I found myself in that part of the city occupied by the Ruthenians.[17] I was a member of the Polish National Committee that convened underground in the building of the Chamber

---

15 Under Russian rule.
16 The full title: Maksymilian Landau, "Materiały do historji artylerji Legjonów Polskich," *Przegląd artyleryjski*, (February 1933): 125; (March 1933): 266.
17 Ukrainians.

of Commerce. There were, among others, [Władysław] Stesłowicz, [Adam T.] Sawczyński, [Marceli] Chłamtacz, and [Count Alexander] Skarbek.

While some of the Jewish population under the Ruthenian occupation proclaimed their "neutrality," we demonstratively represented those Jews who adopted the Polish cause as their own. In such character appeared there, among others, the rector of the [Lwów] university, Prof. [Adolf] Beck, the lawyer [Izydor] Schenker, and I. We were accepted cordially and fraternally.

✏ ✏ ✏

When Polish detachments pushed out the Ruthenians and entered the city, when the white-and-red banner fluttered over the town hall, I was overtaken by enthusiasm. That great moment, for which I longed my whole life, finally came. I decided to immediately enlist for military service. It was then, however, that I received a shock that affected my whole life.

Immediately after the liberation of Lwów, a pogrom against Jews erupted. Complete blocks of houses burned in the Jewish quarter. Drunken marauders strolled through the streets, sacked stores, and plundered apartments. I found a "patrol" in my house: they conducted a "search," holding revolvers aimed at my wife. I was immediately arrested, because on the list of residents was written, next to my surname: "Jewish religion, Polish nationality."

"By what right does this filthy Jew pretend to be a Polish national?!"

Actually, I was immediately released, but instead, my mother was arrested for distributing food to those who lost everything in the fire. She was driven through the street in the midst of insults.

✏ ✏ ✏

Thus, though I used to be unconditionally one of "us," at the time when my feelings were the strongest, I was brutally rejected. Then, as time passed, I relaxed. In a couple of years I voluntarily enlisted in the army and I am a reserve officer. (My son has also enlisted as a volunteer and is an officer as well.) For some time I even served in the consular

129

service. However, this was only wandering on the margins of life. When I looked at these incidents in Lwów from a mitigating historical perspective and again tried to be active, I already was "a stranger" to many.

Such a stigma, although imposed from outside, does not remain without impact on the internal shaping of a man.

I have recently been considering the new direction adopted by the government, which does not quite coincide with my conceptions of political economy. I have suddenly concluded in horror that I was thinking in terms of "them." "They are doing it."

"Why 'they'? Yet, in the past, I always considered such issues as 'us.'"

I have felt that inner reflex, that reflection of the events and moods surrounding me. Nevertheless, I do not actually feel like this! I have not yet changed so much. Yet, despite all that happens, I am aware that our government is fairer than the governments of our neighbors. It does its best for the better future of us all.

That however fleeting—mentioned with horror, and immediately suppressed—manifestation suddenly projected a beam of light on some eerie inner processes and caused the need for contemplation.

తారాతారాతారా

It is not me or my psychical life conflicts that matter. What matters is that not only I, but all Polish Jews, should feel that Poland is "*us*." The point is that Poland should retain that powerful, centuries-old attraction by guaranteeing protection of its citizens and linking them to the state and the nation, thus growing increasingly powerful. The point is that those who widen the differences, cast off the Jews, and wish to build new ghettos—they dwarf Poland.

And insofar as they are able to provoke reflexes, even fleeting reflexes, in the people who are profoundly linked to Poland, how one can be surprised that broad masses which are far removed from the Polish idea, branded by a stigma of hostile otherness, and deterred not only from cooperation but also deprived of every possibility of earning a normal livelihood—are stung by increasingly vitriolic ferment, and the youth has no future, and sometimes, in their hopelessness, are trapped in desperate extremity.

Someone would say that I am an exceptional case, that the masses have always lived in separatism and the Jews who consider themselves as Poles are only a thin stratum that is not decisive about the entire problem.

Such reasoning is fundamentally mistaken, laden with the most fatal consequences. The masses are what they have been shaped by centuries of exclusivist legislation. Only few who grew up in that atmosphere may feel free and equal. The minority's approach is always dependent on the stance adopted toward them by the majority. Hence, the majority should plead guilty if only a relatively thin Jewish stratum managed to nurture an earnest civic consciousness. And it is in the interest of the majority to do everything in order to not only maintain the gained positions, but to broaden the range of influence and ultimately to embrace the whole.

A friend, a former consul of the Polish Republic, has told me that the most sought-after foreign diplomatic posts are those in which there is a large body of Polish Jews. Thus, taking it more or less objectively, wherever, for instance, reside 20,000 such citizens, there will be 20,000 faithful friends and helpers. Jews possess a clear instinct of loyalty and an urge for cooperation where they sense even a bit of fairness and goodwill.

The formula for expansion of Polish loyalty among the Jews is that simple: on the one hand, kind friendliness toward the masses, combined with leniency for the errors instilled in them over the centuries. These errors will soon vanish under the impact of such treatment. On the other hand, it is necessary to invite the cooperation of those individuals who are inspired with the civic consciousness that you intend to develop in the rest of them. Even by their sporadic advancement to the most responsible positions, it would be made clear to the masses that the path to emancipation and to contemporary life standards leads through their impregnation with the state spirit and through service to the state. This way a real rally for Polish identity could be produced among the Jews. To these ends, however, one should work methodically. This was probably [Tadeusz] Kościuszko's mindset. In that manner, Austria, which aroused revolutionary elements among Poles during the period of absolutist rule by Metternich and Stadion, managed to produce later, in the constitutional era, broad spheres of friends and collaborators.

Some may say that a marriage of interests is not worth a lot. Nonetheless, as early as the times of the knights an obligatory principle between the lord and his vassal was loyalty in return for loyalty. The equivalent to the vassal's duties was safety guaranteed by his sovereign. The attitude of the subjects, the attitude of the minority, was almost always a secondary function, dependent on the approach of the suzerain or the majority toward them. Race did not play a role at all. Huguenots were the flesh and blood of France, yet persecutions managed to convert them into fanatic enemies of their own motherland. These refugees served the foes of France; they carried away enormous means of industrial and organizational experience and fashioned a novel economy in Prussia.

Macaulay, in the aforementioned treatise, states correctly:

"If all the red-haired people had been outraged and oppressed in every country, I would not be surprised if a red-haired Englishman would feel more solidarity with a red-haired Portuguese than with a blond or brunet Englishman."[18]

And he draws the right conclusion:

"Every nation has such Jews as they deserve."[19]

Also, in the future they will have such Jews as they will produce.

I am concerned about Poland more than about my co-religionists. Jews have recently survived much and will continue to survive much.

---

18 This sentence is a free paraphrase of Macaulay's wording, see [Macaulay], "Statement of the Civil Disabilities," 369–370.

19 Maucaulay's relevant words are: "The English Jews are, as far as we can see, precisely what our government has made them. They are precisely what any sect,—what any class of men, treated as they have been treated,—would have been" (ibid., 369). The Polish translation mentioned by Lilien accurately follows the original wording; cf. Macaulay, *O Żydach*, 13. The sentence quoted by Lilien corresponds to "Jedes Land hat die Juden, die es verdient," a saying by Karl Emil Franzos, "Todte Seelen," *Neue Freie Presse* (31 March 1875): 2.

Can Poland, however, allow herself an inner weakness instead of a great reinforcement, which she could get in that field?

∽ ∽ ∽

And yet, despite all that is happening, I am looking to the future with optimism. At this moment, two forces are wrestling in Poland. One of them draws its vital forces from the centuries-old traditions of the People, growing out of the depths of the Polish knightly soul, humane and sympathetic, and this very native force consequently leads to a great and just Poland, to the fulfillment of Jagiellonian ideas. The other is a sick acquisition from non-Polish origins. It grew out of the postwar corruption of mores; it originated from the perverse struggle for prey and grub, primitively conceived and inspired from outside by a conscious alien action of foreign agents who defend themselves against the growing and strengthening Polish power.

Temporarily, that force, sustained by strong organization and enormous resources, has gained too much terrain. Yet the struggle goes on. In this fight, we should not lose heart. I have no doubt that, ultimately, the Polish state-building instinct will triumph and the time will come when the present episode will be recollected as a passing nightmare.

Bibliography

Asch, Sholem. *Three Cities*, vol. 3: *Moscow*. London: Victor Gollancz, 1933.

Askenazy, Szymon. *Gdańsk a Polska*. Warsaw: Gebethner i Wolff, 1919.

——. *Książę Józef Poniatowski 1763–1813*. Warsaw: Gebethner i Wolff, 1905.

——. *Napoleon a Polska*. 2 vols. Warsaw: Towarzystwo Wydawnicze, 1918.

Bachowski, Wladysław, and Mieczysław Treter. *Wystawa miniatur i sylwetek we Lwowie 1912*. Lwów: Komitet Wystawy: Gubrynowicz i Syn, 1912.

Bałaban, Majer. *Historia Lwowskiej Synagogi Postępowej*. Lwów: Zarząd Synagogi Postępowej, 1937.

——. *Dzielnica żydowska, jej dzieje i zabytki*. Lwów: Towarzystwo Miłośników Przeszłośći Lwowa, 1909.

——. "Genealogical Tree of the Ornstein-Braude Family" (Heb.). In *Księga jubileuszowa ku czci D-ra Markusa Braudego*, 3–47, plates I–X. Warsaw: Towarzystwo Krzewienia Nauk Judaistycznych w Polsce, 1931.

——. *Żydzi lwowscy na przełomie XVI i XVII wieku*. Lwów: Fundusz konkursowy im. H. Wawelberga, 1906.

Bergner, Matthias, and Karl Märker. "Mises, Edle v." In *Neue Deutsche Biographie*, vol. 17, 563–566. Berlin: Duncker & Humblot, 1994.

Bernstein, Ignatz. *Yiddish Proverbs and Idioms* (Yid.). 2nd ed. Warsaw: Kaufman, 1908.

Bocheński, Adolf Maria. *Między Niemcami a Rosją*. Warsaw: Polityka, 1937.

Brierly, Cornelia. *Tales of Taliesin: A Memoir of Fellowship*. 2nd ed. Rohnert Park, CA: Pomegranate; Frank Lloyd Wright Foundation, 2000.

Bronsen, David. *Joseph Roth: Eine Biographie*. Cologne: Kiepenheuer & Witsch, 1974.

Caillavet, Gaston-Arman de. *La Belle aventure: Comédie en trois actes*. Paris, 1914.

Chołoniewski, Antoni. *Niesmiertelni: Fotografie literatów*. Lwów: n.p., 1898.

Curie, Ève Denise. *Madame Curie: A Biography*. Trans. Vincent Sheean. Garden City, NY: Doubleday, Doran and Co., 1938.

Edelman, Tzvi-Hirsh. *Gdulat Shaul* (Heb.). London: n.p., 1854.

Epler, Adam Józef. *Ostatni żołnierz polski kampanii roku 1939*. London: Wydział Prac Kult.-Ośw. Ministerstwa Obrony Narodowej, 1943.

Feldman, Dmitrii. *Rossiiskie evrei v epokhu napoleonovskikh voin*. Moscow: Drevlekhranilishche, 2013.

Feldman, Dmitrii, and Dmitrii Peters. *Istroriia nagrazhdeniia rossiiskikh evreev za voennye i grazhdanskie zaslugi v nachale XIX veka*. Moscow: Drevlekhranilishche, 2006.

Franzos, Karl Emil. "Todte Seelen." *Neue Freie Presse* 3805 (31 March 1875): 1–3.

Goetel, Ferdynand. "Dyskusja nad problemem żydowskim w Polsce." *Polityka*, 15, no. 161 (10 July 1938): 4–6.

——. *Kar-Chat*. 1922.

——. *Ludzkość*. 1925.

——. *Pątnik Karapeta*. 1921.

——. *Z dnia na dzień*. 1926.

Goldstein, Maksymilian, and Karol Dresdner. *Kultura i sztuka ludu żydowskiego na ziemiach polskich: Zbiory Maksymiliana Goldsteina*. Lwów: M. Goldstein, 1935.

Grinberg, Mikhail, Benjamin Lukin, and Ilia Lurie, eds. *1812 god: Rossia i evrei. Russko-evreiskie istochniki o voine 1812 goda*. Moscow: Gesharim, 2012.

Grobicki, Jerzy. *Bitwa konna pod Jarosławicami 21 sierpnia 1914 r.* Warsaw: Wojskowe Biuro Historyczne, 1930.

Guizot, François Pierre Guillaume. *Mémoires pour servir à l'histoire de mon temps*. 8 vols. Paris: Levy, 1858–1867.

Habielski, Rafał. *Dokąd nam iść wypada? Jerzy Giedroyc od "Buntu Młodych" do "Kultury."* Warsaw: Towarzystwo "Więź," 2007.

Habielski, Rafał, and Jerzy Jaruzelski. *Zamiary, przestrogi, nadzeje: Wybór publicystyki. "Bunt Młodych," "Polityka," 1931–1939.* Lublin: Wydawnictwo Uniwersytetu Marii Curie-Skłodowskiej, 2008.

Harlfinger, R. "Schenk Josef Eduard Frh. von." In *Österreichisches Biographisches Lexikon,* vol. 10, 78–79. Vienna: Verlag der Österreichischen Akademie der Wissenschaften, 1990.

Hoen, Max von, and Egon Waldstätten. *Die letzte Reiterschlacht der Weltgeschichte: Jaroslawice 1914.* Zürich: Amalthea-Verlag, 1929.

Hülsmann, Jörg Guido. *Mises: The Last Knight of Liberalism.* Auburn: Ludwig von Mises Institute, 2007.

Ilustrowany skorowidz stołecznego miasta Lwowa z okazyi Powszechnej Wystawy Krajowej roku 1894. Lwów: Fr. S. Reichman, 1894.

Jakubowski, Józef, et al., eds. *Rocznik polskiego przemysłu i handlu.* Warsaw: Polska spółka wydawnictw informacyjnych, 1936.

Karigl, H. "Schenk Josef Wilhelm Frh. von." In *Österreichisches Biographisches Lexikon,* vol. 10, 79. Vienna: Verlag der Österreichischen Akademie der Wissenschaften, 1990.

Key, Ellen. *Century of the Child.* London: G.P. Putnam's Sons, 1909.

Kowalczuk, Michał. *Cech budowniczy we Lwowie za czasów polskich (do roku 1772).* Lwów: Stowarzyszenie Budowniczych, 1927.

Krasiński, Zygmunt. *Nie-Boska komedia.* Paris: A. Pinard, 1835.

Księga adresowa i informacyjna przedsiębiorstw przemysłowych, handlowych i finansowych w Rzeczypospolitej Polskiej. Warsaw: Izba Przemysłowo-Handlowa, 1930.

Księga adresowa Król. Stoł. Miasta Lwowa. Rocznik 17. 1913; Adress u. Geschäfts-Handbuch von Lemberg. 17. Jg. 1913. Lwów: Fr. Reichman, 1913.

Księga Pamiątkowa Towarzystwa "Bratniej Pomocy" Słuchaczów Politechniki we Lwowie. Lwów: Towarzystwo "Bratniej Pomocy" Słuchaczów Politechniki, 1897.

Landau, Maksymilian. "Materiały do historji artylerji Legjonów Polskich." *Przegląd artyleryjski* (February 1933): 121–146; (March 1933): 257–282.

Lilien, Edward. *Easy Method for Learning Polish Quickly: A New System on the Most Simple Principles for Universal Self-Tuition, with Complete English Pronunciation of Every Word.* New York: Wehman Bros., 1914.

Lilien, Ernest. *Dictionary*, vol. 1. Buffalo: Dziennik dla wszystkich, 1944.

Lilien, Marya. "O Józiu Wittlinie—wspomnienia lwowskiej młodości." *Wiadomości* [London], 25 (November 1979): 3.

Lilien-Brzozdowiecki, Artur. "Garść wspomnień." *Słowo polskie* 169 (21 June 1931): 13.

——. "Myśli polskiego Żyda." *Polityka*, 18, no. 163 (10 August 1938): 6, 8.

——. "Ochrona drobnego akcjonariusza." *Gazeta Bankowa* (25 June 1928): 281–282.

——. "Paneuropa a zagadnienie granic polsko-niemieckich." *Nasza Przyszłość: Wolna trybuna zachowawczej myśli państwowej*, 8 (February 1931): 113–119.

Łoziński, Władysław. *Sztuka lwowska w XVI i XVII wieku: Architektura i rzeźba.* Lwów: H. Altenberg, 1901.

Macaulay, Thomas Babington. *O Żydach.* Trans. K...y M. Lwów: E. Winiarz, 1863.

[Macaulay, Thomas Babington]. "Statement of the Civil Disabilities and Privations Affecting Jews in England." *Edinburgh Review* (January 1831): 363–374.

Malinowski, Jerzy. *Malarstwo i rzeźba Żydów Polskich w XIX i XX wieku.* Warsaw: Wydawnictwo Naukowe PWN, 2000.

Manekin, Rachel. "The Debate over Assimilation in Late Nineteenth-Century Lwów." In *Insiders and Outsiders*, edited by Richard I. Cohen, Jonathan Frankel, and Stefani Hoffman, 120–130. Oxford: Littman Library of Jewish Civilization, 2010.

Maze-Sencier, Alphonse. *Les fournisseurs de Napoléon I.er et des deux impératrices.* Paris: H. Laurens, 1893.

Miszewski, Dariusz. "Polska wobec koncepcji Paneuropy." In *W kręgu polityki*, edited by Adam Ilców and Robert Potocki, 109–118. Zielona Góra: Śląskie Towarzystwo Naukowe im. Michala Grażyńskiego, 2009.

Modelski, Teofil Emil. *Król "Gebalim" w liście Chasdaja: Studyum historyczne z X w.* Lwów: Towarzystwo dla Popierania Nauki Polskiej, 1910.

N. O. Body. *Aus eines Mannes Mädchenjahren.* Berlin: G. Riecke Nachf., 1907.

Nossig, Alfred. *Jan Prorok: Opowieść na tle galicyjskim z 1880 r. w dziewięciu księgach.* Lwów: Księgarnia polska, 1892.

Pappenheim, Bertha. *Sisyphus-Arbeit: Reisebriefe aus den Jahren 1911 und 1912* [1. und] 2. Folge. Leipzig [2.F.: Berlin]: Linder [2.F.: Levy], 1929.

Pappenheim, Bertha, and David Kaufmann. *Die Memoiren der Glückel von Hameln: geboren in Hamburg 1645, gestorben in Metz 19. September 1724.* Vienna: Verlag von S. Meyer und W. Pappenhiem, 1910.

Polski przemysł i handel: Rynek polski; Księga adresowa i informacyjna przedsiębiorstw przemysłowych, handlowych i finansowych w Rzeczypospolitej Polskiej. Warsaw: Izba Przemysłowo-Handlowa, 1930.

Préaud, Tamara. "Les 'grands hommes' en sculptures à Sèvres au XIXème siècle." *The French Porcelain Society Journal* 2 (2005): 120–132.

Pytel, R. "Mises Majer Jerachmiel von." In *Österreichisches Biographisches Lexikon*, vol. 6, 317. Graz: H. Böhlau, 1975.

Rabelais, François. *La plaisante, et ioyeuse histoyre du grand geant Gargantua.* 3 vols. Geneva[?], ca. 1600.

Raczyński, Edward. *Dziennik podróży do Turcyi odbytej w roku 1814.* Wrocław: W.B. Korn, 1823.

Rej, Mikołaj. *Źwierciadło, albo Kształt, w którym każdy stan snadnie się może swym sprawam jako we źwierciedle przypatrzyć.* Kraków, 1567–1568.

Rich, Merney. "Marya Lilien: Frank Lloyd Wright Opened My Mind." *Chicago Tribune* (15 May 1988), section 6, 3.

Rosenfeld, Morris. *Lieder des Ghetto.* Trans. from the Yiddish by Berthold Feiwel with drawings by E. M. Lilien. Berlin: B. Harz, 1902.

Rosenthal, Herman. "Bernstein, Ignacy." In *The Jewish Encyclopedia*, vol. 3, 100. New York: Funk & Wagnalls, 1903.

Roth, Joseph. *Briefe 1911–1934*. Edited by Hermann Kesten. Cologne: Kiepenheuer & Witsch, 1970.

———. *Hotel Savoy; Fallmerayer the Stationmaster; The Bust of the Emperor.* Translated by John Hoare. Woodstock: Overlook Press, 1986.

———. *A Life in Letters*. Translated and edited by Michael Hofmann. New York: W. W. Norton & Co., 2012.

Rothschild, Joseph. *East Central Europe between the Two World Wars.* Seattle: University of Washington Press, 1974.

Rozenblit, Marsha L. "Jewish Identity and the Modern Rabbi: The Cases of Isak Noa Mannheimer, Adolf Jellinek, and Moritz Güdemann in Nineteenth-Century Vienna." *Leo Baeck Institute Year Book* 35 (1990): 103–131.

Samuel, B. "Helene von Mises." *Ost und West* 12 (December 1905): 787–792.

Sapieha, Leon. *Wspomnienia*. Kraków: G. Gebethner i Spółka, 1912.

Skarga, Piotr. *Żywoty świętych*. Wilno: Mikołaj Krzysztof Radziwiłł, 1579.

Skorowidz adresowy król. stoł. miasta Lwowa. Rocznik 2. Rok 1910. Lwów: Jan Rudolf Spigel, 1910.

Stahl, Zdzisław. *Zbrodnia Katyńska w świetle dokumentów*. London: "Gryf," 1950.

Stande, Stanisław Ryszard. *Rzeczy i ludzie*. Krakow: Drukarnia Narodowa, 1925.

———. *Molodezh' idet*. Moscow: OGIZ, 1933.

———. *Stikhi*. Moscow: Litizdat, 1935.

Śleszyński, Wojciech. *Obóz odosobnienia w Berezie Kartuskiej 1934–39.* Białystok: Instytut Historii Uniwersytetu w Bialymstoku, 2003.

Teslar, Józef Andrzej. "Rozmowy z Janem." *Wiadomości Polskie* [London] (30 January 1944): 1.

Vauban, Sébastien Le Prestre de, et al. *Maniere de fortifier de Mr. de Vauban: Où l'on voit de quelle méthode on se sert aujourd'hui en France, pour la fortification des places tant régulieres qu'irréguliers; En quoi cette méthode differe des autres, &c.: avec un traité de geometrie qu'on a mis à la tête, pour avoir une parfaite intelligence des fortifications.* Amsterdam, 1689.

Vuitsyk, Volodymyr. "Ploshcha Rynok, 18." *Visnyk instytutu Ukrzak-hidproektrestavratsiia* 14 (2004): 123–126.

Wierzbianski, Boleslaw, ed. "Lilien, Marya de Czarnecka." In *Who's Who in Polish America: 1996–1997*, 262. New York: Bicentennial Pub. Corp., 1996.

Wyspiański, Stanisław. *Wesele: dramat w 3 aktach*. Kraków: Stanisław Wyspiański, 1901.

Zdrada, J. "Mises Herman von, publizist und politiker." In *Österreichisches Biographisches Lexikon*, vol. 6, 317. Graz: H. Böhlau, 1975.

Żakowicz, Aleksander. *Fotografia galicyjska do roku 1918: Fotografowie Galicji, Tatr oraz Księstwa Cieszyńskiego*. Lwów: "Centrum Europy," 2008.

Żuławski, Jerzy. *Eros i Psyche, Powieść sceniczna w siedmiu rozdziałach*. Lwów: H. Altenberg, 1904.

Żygulski, Zdzisław Jun. "Ze Lwowa do Chicago: Wspomnienie o Marii Lilien-Czarneckiej." *Cracovia Leopolis* 2 (2005): 14–17.

Index